exploring

HEAVENLY PLACES

The Power of God, on Earth as it is in Heaven

VOLUME V

PAUL L. COX
BARBARA KAIN PARKER

EXPLORING HEAVENLY PLACES
The Power of God, on Earth as it is in Heaven

VOLUME V
Paul L. Cox and Barbara Kain Parker

Aslan's Place Publications
9315 Sagebrush Street
Apple Valley, CA 92308
760-810-0990

www.aslansplace.com

Unless otherwise noted, all scripture quotations are from the New King James Version of the Bible. Copyright © 1979, 1980, 1982 by Thomas Nelson, Inc., publishers. Used by permission.

Greek definitions are derived from *Strong's Greek Concordance*.
Hebrew definitions are derived from *Strong's Hebrew Concordance*.

TABLE OF CONTENTS

INTRODUCTION 4

CHAPTER 1: *Pondering The Power Of God* 7

CHAPTER 2: *Power, On Earth As It Is In Heaven* 12

CHAPTER 3: *The Gift Of Tongues* 16

CHAPTER 4: *Tongues Of Men And Angels* 27

CHAPTER 5: *Power For Living, Power For Dying* 34

CHAPTER 6: *Unfolding Revelation Of God's Power* 42

CHAPTER 7: *Puzzling Pieces Of Revelation* 47

CHAPTER 8: *The Missing Piece* 57

CHAPTER 9: *Breakthrough* 65

CHAPTER 10: *The Golden Pipes* 71

CHAPTER 11: *Windows And Branches* 80

CHAPTER 12: *Prayer Renouncing Illegal Access
                Of The Windows Of Heaven* 85

CHAPTER 13: *The Greatest Power* 90

ENDNOTES 98

INTRODUCTION

The highly anticipated *Star Wars: The Force Awakens* was recently released, much to joy of innumerable fans. The combination of old and new characters, a riveting story line, and state-of-the-art special effects kept moviegoers glued to the edge of their seats. The film quickly set box office records, and even people who don't usually care for such movies are often heard to say that they enjoyed this one.

Meanwhile, another Force; One who has never needed to awaken because He has never slept; One who is more powerful than anything the most talented screenwriters could contrive; has been revealing astonishing new aspects of His Power.[1] The Creator of all those stars, and everything else that exists for that matter, makes it clear that His Force really is something to be reckoned with, and as we experience His Power we go way beyond the imagination of mankind.

Exploring Heavenly Places, Volume 5 continues to examine the manifestations of God's power that originate in heavenly places and manifest here on the earth. Even as we write, we can relate to the Apostle John's words:

> *And there are also many other things that Jesus did, which if they were written one by one, I suppose that even the world itself could not contain the books that would be written.*[2]

God is setting such a rapid pace for illuminating new levels of spiritual understanding that it's hard to keep up, and it's clear that we will never be able to write everything that God wants to share about Himself and His creation—He will always have more to reveal. Even as the previous book was being edited, there was already new revelation that will be integrated into this volume, and as this introduction is being written we already have enough content for several new volumes in the series. Please remember that everything we present has been developed within a community of believers, with individuals discerning and exploring together the mysteries being unwrapped by Holy Spirit. As you read, it is our prayer:

> ...*that the God of our Lord Jesus Christ, the Father of glory, may give to you the spirit of wisdom and revelation in the knowledge of Him, the eyes of your understanding being enlightened; that you may know what is the hope of His calling, what are the riches of the glory of His inheritance in the saints, and what is the exceeding greatness of His power toward us who believe, according to the working of His mighty power which He worked in Christ when He raised Him from the dead and seated Him at His right hand in the heavenly places, far above all principality and power and might and dominion, and every name that is named, not only in this age but also in that which is to come.*[3]

CHAPTER ONE

Pondering the Power of God

There are a plethora of wonderful old gospel songs that sing of the glory to be witnessed in heaven, but we don't have to wait until we die to experience His glorious Presence and Power here on earth. The "sweet bye-and-bye" will indeed be wonderful, but how much better it is to be able to experience Him in the here-and-now.

God's Power is evident throughout the Old Testament; from creation to Israel's deliverance from Pharaoh, to the cloud by day and the pillar of fire by night, to the manna and the water from a rock that He provided for His own. In those early days of Israel, God's Power resided within the Ark of the Covenant; a lesson the Philistines learned all too well, much to their chagrin:

> *Then the Philistines took the ark of God and brought it from Ebenezer to Ashdod. When the Philistines took the ark of God, they brought it into the house of Dagon and set it by Dagon. And when the people of Ashdod arose early in the morning, there was Dagon, fallen on its face to the earth before the ark of the Lord. So they took Dagon and set it in its place again. And when they arose early the next morning, there was Dagon, fallen on its face to the ground before the ark of the Lord. The head of Dagon and both the*

palms of its hands were broken off on the threshold; only Dagon's torso was left of it...But the hand of the Lord was heavy on the people of Ashdod, and He ravaged them and struck them with tumors, both Ashdod and its territory. And when the men of Ashdod saw how it was, they said, "The ark of the God of Israel must not remain with us, for His hand is harsh toward us and Dagon our god." Therefore they sent and gathered to themselves all the lords of the Philistines, and said, "What shall we do with the ark of the God of Israel?" And they answered, "Let the ark of the God of Israel be carried away to Gath." So they carried the ark of the God of Israel away. So it was, after they had carried it away, that the hand of the Lord was against the city with a very great destruction; and He struck the men of the city, both small and great, and tumors broke out on them. Therefore they sent the ark of God to Ekron. So it was, as the ark of God came to Ekron, that the Ekronites cried out, saying, "They have brought the ark of the God of Israel to us, to kill us and our people!" So they sent and gathered together all the lords of the Philistines, and said, "Send away the ark of the God of Israel, and let it go back to its own place, so that it does not kill us and our people." For there was a deadly destruction throughout all the city; the hand of God was very heavy there. And the men who did not die were stricken with the tumors, and the cry of the city went up to heaven.[1]

The Godless Philistines recognized the Power of God and, in desperation, sent the Ark back to the Israelites loaded with gifts, seemingly hoping against hope that it would be enough:

Then take the ark of the Lord and set it on the cart; and put the articles of gold which you are returning to Him as a trespass offering in a chest by its side. Then send it away, and let it go. And watch: if it goes up the road to its own territory, to Beth Shemesh, then He has done us this great evil. But if not, then we shall know that it is not His hand that struck us—it happened to us by chance.[2]

The Israelites rejoiced to see the Ark coming along the road and, using the wood from the cart for the fire, they offered the two cows that had been pulling it as a burnt offering. It was definitely time for praise and worship! Unfortunately though, many of them forgot how sacred the glory of the Lord is; they forgot about the honor and respect that was required by God:

> *Then He struck the men of Beth Shemesh, because they had looked into the ark of the Lord. He struck fifty thousand and seventy men of the people, and the people lamented because the Lord had struck the people with a great slaughter. And the men of Beth Shemesh said, "Who is able to stand before this holy Lord God? And to whom shall it go up from us?"[3]*

About twenty years later, King David and the Israelites had to re-learn that very hard lesson about God's Power when Uzzah was struck dead for simply reaching out to steady the Ark with his hand. At first glance it may seem a harsh action by God, but it happened because the proper respect was not being paid to Him, and the Ark was being moved in a manner that may have been convenient but had nothing in common with God's instructions.[4]

Unlike those early days before Jesus came, the kingdom of God no longer resides within the Ark, but within His people, which means that the kingdom of God is already here and is accessible:

> *Now when He was asked by the Pharisees when the kingdom of God would come, He answered them and said, "The kingdom of God does not come with observation; nor will they say, 'See here!' or 'See there!' For indeed, the kingdom of God is within you."[5]*

> *But if I cast out demons by the Spirit of God, surely the kingdom of God has come upon you.[6]*

> *Then Jesus answered and said to them, "Most assuredly, I say to you, the Son can do nothing of Himself, but what He sees the Father do; for whatever He does, the Son also does in like manner.[7]*

> *For I have not spoken on My own authority; but the Father who sent Me gave Me a command, what I should say and what I should speak.[8]*

Surely Jesus was different though, right? Wrong! Jesus set aside His position as God and operated here on earth as any other man would. As is evident in the verses above, He tuned into His Father for direction, and one miracle after another provides evidence that it was the Power of God that raised the dead, healed the sick, cast out demons, and transformed lives:

> *Then Jesus returned in the power of the Spirit to Galilee, and news of Him went out through all the surrounding region.*[9]

> *Then they were all amazed and spoke among themselves, saying, "What a word this is! For with authority and power He commands the unclean spirits, and they come out."*[10]

> *Now it happened on a certain day, as He was teaching, that there were Pharisees and teachers of the law sitting by, who had come out of every town of Galilee, Judea, and Jerusalem. And the power of the Lord was present to heal them.*[11]

How then, can we doubt that such Power is available today when Jesus Himself declared:

> *Most assuredly, I say to you, he who believes in Me, the works that I do he will do also; and greater works than these he will do, because I go to My Father.*[12]

> *But you shall receive power when the Holy Spirit has come upon you; and you shall be witnesses to Me in Jerusalem, and in all Judea and Samaria, and to the end of the earth.*[13]

It is clear that we can experience the Power of God now and don't have to wait until we all get to Heaven. However, we'd be wise to remember those poor old Philistines, the fifty-thousand-and-seventy, and Uzzah. We cannot touch God's glory; it's His and His alone, and when His Power manifests on earth, we'd better remember to respect, fear and acknowledge Him, and never try to claim any of His glory for ourselves.

The words of the Apostle Paul summarize well:

> *I became a minister according to the gift of the grace of God given to me by the effective working of His power.*[14]

> *Now to Him who is able to do exceedingly abundantly above all that we ask or think, according to the power that works in us, to Him be glory in the church by Christ Jesus to all generations, forever and ever. Amen.*[15]

CHAPTER TWO

Power, On Earth as it is in Heaven

As is obvious from the title, this book series explores heavenly places, and much of what we've written thus far may have seemed pretty far out in terms of the usual way of thinking. We've spoken of heavenly experiences that occur in dimensions that exist beyond our normal everyday perceptions, quite a stretch for some of our minds. As we write about dimensions of height, depth, width and height, the grid, spiritual gates and doors, spiritual stars, etc., our thoughts naturally run to a type of *Star Wars* mindset, which focuses on dimensions and galaxies far, far away. However, the dimensional heavenly places can also be very close at hand. I (Barbara) have come to appreciate, and often share, Paul's frequent assertion that we are actually much bigger inside than we are outside. We need to learn to think dimensionally, for our existence is not confined to the physical realm:

> *Or do you not know that your body is the temple of the Holy Spirit who is in you, whom you have from God, and you are not your own?*[1]

Again, the kingdom of heaven is like treasure hidden in a field, which a man found and hid; and for joy over it he goes and sells all that he has and buys that field.[2]

Now when He was asked by the Pharisees when the kingdom of God would come, He answered them and said, "The kingdom of God does not come with observation; nor will they say, 'See here!' or 'See there!' For indeed, the kingdom of God is within you."[3]

We frequently read and pray the Lord's Prayer,[4] but how often do we stop and consider the magnitude of the fact that His kingdom is already here? It's so easy to simply assume that *on earth as it is in heaven* is future tense, and will become evident in the millennial kingdom when Jesus literally returns to rule and reign from His throne in Jerusalem. In reality, His kingdom, spoken of by John the Baptist, has already come:

In those days John the Baptist came preaching in the wilderness of Judea, and saying, "Repent, for the kingdom of heaven is at hand!" For this is he who was spoken of by the prophet Isaiah, saying:

> *"The voice of one crying in the wilderness:*
> *'Prepare the way of the Lord;*
> *Make His paths straight.'"*[5]

And He said to them, "Assuredly, I say to you that there are some standing here who will not taste death till they see the kingdom of God present with power."[6]

Many manifestations of God's miraculous Power on earth are so common that I fear we may easily take them for granted. It seems to be a fact of life that we soon begin to undervalue that which we have been freely given or become too familiar with. Jesus understood, and He illustrated this principle when He said:

A prophet is not without honor except in his own country, among his own relatives, and in his own house.[7]

We are familiar with such concepts as salvation, healing, deliverance, and answered prayer; we speak freely about dreams and visions; but how often do we stop to consider the Power of God that makes each of these possible?

> *For I am not ashamed of the gospel of Christ, for it is the power of God to salvation for everyone who believes, for the Jew first and also for the Greek.*[8]

> *And when He had called His twelve disciples to Him, He gave them power over unclean spirits, to cast them out, and to heal all kinds of sickness and all kinds of disease.*[9]

> *Then He appointed twelve, that they might be with Him and that He might send them out to preach, and to have power to heal sicknesses and to cast out demons:*[10]

We also love to speak of the gifts of the Spirit and the fruit of the Spirit, but do we realize the magnitude of Power behind them? In reality, we experience the dimensional manifestations of His Power every day, but it is so familiar that we don't realize that we are already exploring heavenly places or, perhaps, we've just never thought of it that way. Consider hope, joy and peace, for example; they sound so soothing and nice, but they are available only through the Power of God, and they do not exist in the natural:

> *...for the kingdom of God is not eating and drinking, but righteousness and peace and joy in the Holy Spirit.*[11]

> *Now may the God of hope fill you with all joy and peace in believing, that you may abound in hope by the power of the Holy Spirit.*[12]

Jesus is our all-time best example of how to live and think dimensionally because His physical existence on earth was just like ours. Having set aside His deity and totally dependent on His Father, though bodily confined to the physical realm He accessed the heavenly places through the Power of the Holy Spirit. The

Apostle Paul understood this, and his words to the philosophers of Athens echo the reality of the God in whom we exist:

> *God, who made the world and everything in it, since He is Lord of heaven and earth, does not dwell in temples made with hands…And He has made [man]…so that they should seek the Lord, in the hope that they might grope for Him and find Him, though He is not far from each one of us; for in Him we live and move and have our being…*[13]

As we explore the kingdom on earth as it is in heaven, we would also do well to remember some other words of Jesus, words that are very familiar, words that have everything to do with Power and His kingdom's existence in the here and now:

> *And I will pray the Father, and He will give you another Helper, that He may abide with you forever—the Spirit of truth, whom the world cannot receive, because it neither sees Him nor knows Him; but you know Him, for He dwells with you and will be in you. I will not leave you orphans; I will come to you. A little while longer and the world will see Me no more, but you will see Me. Because I live, you will live also. At that day you will know that I am in My Father, and you in Me, and I in you. He who has My commandments and keeps them, it is he who loves Me. And he who loves Me will be loved by My Father, and I will love him and manifest Myself to him.*[14]

CHAPTER THREE

The Gift of Tongues

The gift of tongues is a common manifestation of God's Power on earth. On one hand, many dedicated Christians believe the gifts stopped with the early church, thus denying this aspect of Power altogether. On the other hand, more charismatic believers readily embrace tongues, but the gift is so familiar and normal that I (Barbara) doubt it is often recognized as the amazing evidence of God's Power that it is, a gift that is only available through the Holy Spirit:

And they were all filled with the Holy Spirit and began to speak with other tongues, as the Spirit gave them utterance.[1]

> *In the law it is written: "With men of other tongues and other lips I will speak to this people; And yet, for all that, they will not hear Me," says the Lord. Therefore tongues are for a sign, not to those who believe but to unbelievers; but prophesying is not for unbelievers but for those who believe.[2]*

When we meet to discern and explore the mysteries of God, angels often come with messages and some are initially delivered in tongues, which Paul discerns. In his words:

> I was a Baptist after all! The gift of tongues was not in the paradigm of my belief system.

> After the Holy Spirit came with Power in 1991, I often pondered if I would get the gift of tongues. Many would pray for me to receive the gift but nothing happened. It was not until sometime in the middle 1990's that I experienced a drastic change. I was awakened one night with the awareness of a huge territorial spirit coming against me. As I went into the living room, I realized that I was not making any progress against the spirit. Suddenly, I started speaking in tongues and the attack evaporated. The gift of tongues had exploded upon me.

> As I matured in the gift of tongues I realized that I could discern whether a person's tongue was from God or from the enemy. I would put my hand over the person's mouth as they spoke in tongues and could tell if the presence of God was there. If I discerned evil, I would have the person ask the Lord to remove all demonic tongues and then there would be a free flow of the Holy Spirit.

> I first discerned the person of the Holy Spirit in December 2012. Then, a couple of years later, I began to feel in the center of my discernment of the Holy Spirit a small updraft of anointing. This spot on the left back part of my head would continue for many minutes. I had a sense from the Lord that I was discerning a tongue as a righteous spiritual being. I would pray in tongues for a few moments and the sensation would disappear.

> As I was conducting meetings, I would experience the same sensation and would know that someone would

have a tongue. After the tongue was released, the sensation would end, and then it would begin again. I knew there was a spiritual being bringing the interpretation.[3] When the interpretation had concluded I would no longer have the impression of the tongue/interpretation. This understanding has brought much order to our meetings, as we are aware of when the Lord desires to speak to us in tongues.

Paul may also hear a specific tone that indicates to him that angels are singing:

Sing to the Lord, all the earth; Proclaim the good news of His salvation from day to day.[4]

When a tongue is presented, we always follow the scriptural admonition that a public tongue must be interpreted,[5] so we wait for it. Either the person with the tongue or someone else may receive the interpretation. When I (Barbara) have felt an interpretation downloading, it has felt like a whoosh coming down over my head, as if something was being poured out.

During a webinar in October 2015,[6] the interpretation of a tongue was given to a young man named Tony, who had never experienced such a thing before. It was also his very first visit to Aslan's Place, yet he bravely agreed to try to understand the message. The conversation that occurred as Paul gently taught Tony to listen and hear the interpretation serves as a great lesson for all. Paul first discerned that an angel had placed a hand on Tony's head:

(Paul) I want you to try something that may be very difficult for you.

(Tony) OK.

(Paul) I want you to see if you have any thoughts, and tell us what they are. If you can't do that, it's fine because this is called *Exploring Heavenly Places* and we're doing that—just exploring.

(Tony) So what am I going to try to do?

(Paul) Try to listen to the angel. Why don't you start with the scripture that you got a few minutes ago?

(Tony) Yeah, I thought it might be relevant. It's 2 Peter 3:10:

> *He who would love life*
> *And see good days,*
> *Let him refrain his tongue from evil,*
> *And his lips from speaking deceit.*

(Paul) Now, listen to see what else you get. It may be like a thought coming into your head.

(Tony) Should I close my eyes?

(Paul) Whatever is easiest for you to discern. Lord, we ask You to deliver the message. Tony, you're a very brave man!

(Tony) I'm desperate! [He laughs.] But nothing's coming yet.

(Paul) It actually says in the Bible, "Blessed are those who wait on the Lord." It may be just one word at first. Pray, "Lord, I just want one word."

(Brian Cox)[7] I just want to point out that you want to have all of your senses open. You might see something— for instance, a scroll in front of you. Or, you might hear something or see a picture in your mind. What's interesting is that the gift of the prophetic isn't just spoken information from God, so be ready for something

19

to change in what you're thinking about or what you see; and when I say, "see" it may not be blatantly right in front of you, but could be in your mind's eye. We constantly practice this; it doesn't necessarily come automatically, though it could. Just be ready for any new information, and then we will test whatever you get.

(Paul) Now, something interesting is happening. Initially the angel had its hand on Tony's forehead, but now it's over his eyes.

(Tony) I have a question. Was it on my head or my forehead?

(Paul) You may feel the angel's presence on top of your head, as I do, but when I put my hand at your forehead I can feel that his hand has moved to your eyes. By the way, I'm really proud of you—this is amazing!

Paul asks Jana Green,[8] who often receives angelic messages and interpretation of tongues, to stand with Tony and pray for him.

(Paul) We've never done this before with a new guy. OK, here it comes, and it feels like the flow of the river. Let's just wait on the Lord for a minute.

Tobias Renken,[9] participating online from Germany, points out that Paul's discernment of the shift of the angel's hand position may indicate the Lord was shifting Tony's primary gifting from that of teacher to prophet.[10] Paul checked and confirmed that is exactly what had happened, and that Tony's prophetic gifting had been activated.

(Tony) I smell roses. Is anyone wearing rose perfume?

(Paul) The smell just showed up.

(Tony) So there are no roses here, right? Thank you Lord, for this time together and for letting me smell roses. There's got to be more.

(Paul, smiling) He liked it when you said that! Lord, I release Tony and give him permission to speak Your word here in this place today. Lord, I pull him into the fullness of what You have for him right now [holding Tony's arms, he physically pulled him a few steps forward, symbolizing the spiritual movement].

(Tony) Father, if there's a word that You would share with us here, please give it to any one of us or help me to hear You speak it.

(Paul) You're having a teaching moment here for everybody, for there are probably a lot of people watching who also find it difficult to hear. The Lord wants to cause breakthrough I think. You may not get it, but you are really trying. What are you feeling right now?

(Tony) Well, physically I'm hot, and my heart's a little fast, but I was preparing to come here so this is my third day fasting. I thought I'd be more sensitive, but I have no idea if that's the case.

(Paul) Absolutely! Evidently, that's one reason why you're standing here right now...I kept wondering, "Why is the Lord picking on you?" Jana and others also thought that you are the one with the interpretation, and you have to understand that we don't ordinarily do this!

(Tony) Yeah, I know. I watched about fourteen hours of Aslan's Place stuff so...

(Brian) I just want to point out that your demonstration of obedience may actually be part of the message that God wanted to send. I know that things here can go so fast that people may get discouraged, as if on a train that's already going seventy miles per hour, but I believe God is saying; and I hope I'm not jumping on your word; that everyone has to start somewhere, and so what you're demonstrating is the beginning in this.

(Paul) That was an excellent word! Say that again.

(Brian) Everyone has to start somewhere.

(Paul) That's part of the word everybody—that's excellent!

(Tony) Well, I did have an experience four weeks ago that...

(Paul) Now, wait a minute. When you said that I felt an anointing. Sometimes the word just seems to be so obvious, but I remember that early on I heard a profound thing; in the prophetic you sometimes say the obvious, but there is a spiritual push behind the words making them greater than what you'd ordinarily say. So, share that experience.

(Tony) Four weeks ago I went to a conference in Arizona, and four different prophetic words were spoken over me that were very accurate, but one thing was really unique. Two intercessors were praying for me because we'd been talking about the baptism of the Holy Spirit. I'd been seeking the baptism of the Holy Spirit for three years and I'd brought it up because of an experience three years ago. I get sleep paralysis and sometimes I see frightening things while coming in and out of sleep. This time it was different and though I was locked down, I saw a flash of light and felt praises swelling up in my belly; coming up, coming up, coming up; and I had to, wanted to, pray. Half awake, I could see the room but my body was not moving and I started speaking, releasing it. Then my wife was poking me because usually when I'm mumbling like that I want her to wake me up; but I was like, I think it's the Holy Spirit; stop; don't wake me up, don't wake me up! After that day—I guess I'll be really blunt—I had a lot of issues with a certain type of people who live an immoral lifestyle, and it made me very angry when I'd see them, but a few days later I saw someone like that and I immediately had compassion. I'd never experienced that kind of compassion before, and I heard a very cliché word, "Jesus died for them too," which I hear all of the time, but it hadn't meant much to me. So anyway, fast-forward to four weeks ago as these people prayed for me and my tongue started, but I was not going to fake it!

(Paul) Good for you!

(Tony) Other people may think it's real, but I need to know it's real. My tongue started flapping, using a muscle in my tongue I never knew was there—it's underneath my tongue and I never thought of using it before. It started going really strong and they started prophesying over me, giving accurate words. The cool part was that the day before a guy had said to sharpen my sword, and not get caught off guard because a shift would happen very quickly. So, as they were praying for me, I was wondering if the sword was the Word of God when the lady who was praying said, "I'm going to put a sword into your hand." I was thinking, "Here it comes, but I'm not going to fake anything." The moment the sword touched my hand, though I didn't feel the sword I did feel a surge of praise go up through my arm and out through my mouth. My eyes were closed and I felt a finger poke my belly, and another sword of praise came out. Later, I asked if they'd poked me and they said no, but I physically felt someone poke me.

(Paul) OK. That was the word.

(Tony, surprised) That was the word?

(Paul) That was the word. So, you had the thought to go back to what happened four weeks ago, and that was what you were supposed to say. I don't feel the angel there anymore. Now, see how different that is, but what do we usually do? We think that we're getting our own thoughts, but remember that Isaiah said, *"Everything I have accomplished, You have done for me."* [11] God was in what you said and this was a God moment, though you think you're just sharing an experience. So why did He want you to share that experience? Because that's what needed to be said. Isn't that weird?

(Tony) Yeah, it is!

(Paul) I'll tell you, as you were sharing that memory I felt that it had been written in a book.

(Jana) The Book of Remembrance.[12]

(Paul) Oh, the anointing! Can you feel that? Something was taken from the book of your life and you shared it.

(Tony) That's cool.

(Paul) It is cool, and it wasn't a prophetic word, so this is brand new. You see; we had to have someone brand new to do something brand new. OK, I think that's it.

(Tony) Thank you.

(Paul) No, thank you! Aren't we glad that he did this? It is an important reminder for prayer ministry that as we listen, the Lord will bring to remembrance those issues in our life and generational line that He wants us to examine.

(Brian) An online participant confirmed that just as Paul said, "That was the word," he heard the same thing.

Those of us viewing this exchange were certainly blessed, but it is now obvious that God had an even bigger reason for it. Who else would know at the time that it would fit so perfectly into this textual account about tongues that wouldn't be written, or even considered, for another four months? Our Lord certainly does all things well, for the exchange with Tony not only provided the perfect teaching opportunity about learning to listen for an interpretation, but his personal account also emphasized the truth that a tongue is a Holy Spirit-given gift that cannot be faked. Tony's testimony is also a wonderful illustration that God is perfectly capable of working in/through his children even before they receive His gift of tongues.

I thank my God I speak with tongues more than you all; yet in the church I would rather speak five words with my understanding, that I may teach others also, than ten thousand words in a tongue.[13]

Like Paul, "I (Barbara) was a Baptist after all!" So when the Lord started speaking to me about tongues, I was pretty intimidated and wasn't at all sure I wanted that gift! Knowing it was something that would not be accepted by many of my friends and family, I argued with Him for several weeks, but my desire to be obedient eventually won out and I told Him, "OK", but made it clear I needed to know for certain that it was of Him and not my own imagination. He was kind and gentle, and started me out slowly with just a few words that soon became a few phrases. Still, I agonized over whether they were His words or my imagination. One day I realized there was a pattern, and that there was one particular letter in our alphabet that was never used. Soon afterward, as I was speaking in tongues one day, the letter popped up in a word I spoke and I realized immediately that it was false. It was His proof to me that He would show me how to tell the difference, and as my trust in Him to sanctify His gift grew, the phrases soon became a language and, on occasion, several different languages. Interestingly enough though, I'd been serving the Lord for over forty years without the gift, so I've had quite a problem with the common belief of some that one cannot move in or be used by the Holy Spirit without the gift of tongues.

Paul shares his own experience:

> I did deliverances for years and never spoke in tongues. I had a guy said that you can't do that without speaking in tongues. I said, "Well, I guess God doesn't know that." It was sometime in 1997-98 when I was fighting some territorial stuff, and dealing with new issues at night. I was up and on the phone when, all of a sudden, bammmm, and I started speaking in tongues and the thing I was battling left. This is nice; this works; and since then I've spoken in tongues; but for four or five years, I did deliverances and didn't speak in tongues. I wonder how God did that without my speaking in tongues?

The answer to Paul's question is pretty obvious. Tongues are a wonderful spiritual gift, but they are just that—a gift. They do not illustrate our own abilities or strengths, but are evidence of God's Power, manifested on earth as it is in heaven.

CHAPTER FOUR

Tongues of Men and Angels

During a trip to Minnesota in September 2015, we had been exploring the impact that abortion plays in affirming a covenant of death[1] in the USA when an angel arrived. Paul sensed it was there to renew the covenant of life, and that its message would come in the form of an angelic tongue, which is quite different than the tongues most of us are used to hearing. Perhaps, like me (Barbara), you haven't previously considered the idea than an angel's tongue might be different than those we are so used to hearing, but angelic tongues are quite unique. They all seem to be very joyous and musical, the sound often reminiscent of birds singing to one another, and the angelic joy is likely to spill over as smiles and laughter among the listeners. It's clear that it is biblical:

> *Though I speak with the tongues of men and of angels, but have not love, I have become sounding brass or a clanging cymbal.*[2]

In this case, a lady bravely agreed to try to receive and deliver the angelic tongue, and my immediate sense when she began to speak was that she was indeed calling out to a larger audience of angels, joyfully urging them to come and get in on the celebration. Another participant gave the following translation of the angel's tongue:

> You are entering a new season; I am calling in a new season; I am releasing the angel of fire; I am releasing new levels and new dimensions, new giftings that have been held up…(sees bunches of keys coming down and being placed in our hands)…I've made you gatekeepers. I've made you to shut doors and open doors of which you have said, "I can't do this today," but you can do this. Do not wait for others…I'm releasing keys, keys to open and shut, new eyes and new ears.

As the angelic tongue was spoken, someone saw light coming out of the lady's mouth while, at the same time, black capes were coming off of people, as if the breath of God were blowing away a blackness that represented death's covenant. Another lady saw a hand motion and a shofar being raised, and said that the person who released a tongue was the voice of the shofar.

Another aspect of tongues is that they may be written. A young man, who has participated at Aslan's Place, writes tongues in a text that looks similar to Hebrew, with letters that are written from right to left. Paul can discern the Lord's anointing on the paper. The first time I was in a meeting with him, the young man began passing me notes, and with each one I would immediately get a scripture as the interpretation, which then played into our discussion. On other occasions, people have been able to read his written tongues, one of which was the inscription above a spiritual gate. An exchange from that discernment session not only illustrates one such word, but also the fun we have as we meet together to explore the heavenly places:

> (Paul) OK, here we have a tongue that has been written, and it's up on a gate. It's a little different than we've seen before. How in the world does he do that? Look at that. How do you do that? You see that Tobias? Hey, Tobias

(who is online in Germany), I think it would be fun for you to try and translate this.

(Tobias) It's not German, Paul.

(Paul) No, it's not. You're really quick.

A short discussion ensues about the gate, some scriptures come to mind, and then the interpretation of the written tongue is received.

(Tobias) Look to the east, not to the west; revelation is coming from the east; something about new hope and new boundaries. I see a ship coming from the east…a new strength arising in the bones. I saw bones getting together and getting up and the meat, the flesh, coming onto them like in Ezekiel… and I hear that the strength is coming from the west, but the revelation is coming from the east and they have to meet.

In May 2014, both Paul and Jana Green experienced tongues in a new way, and the fun we enjoy during exploration is also evident in this conversation. A young lady had just given an interpretation but Paul was still hearing angels singing, which meant that there was more to the message:

(Jana) I have a whole new thing going on here; I am watching the tongue. It is literally nuts.

(Paul) Well, tell us.

(Jana) It looks like grapes that gather together. I mean; it's more than one angel speaking. It's for us.

(Paul) So can you give it?

Jana spoke in tongues.

(Paul) OK. I don't hear the singing anymore. Oh! Oh my word, I'm hearing the interpretation as a sound. This is new. Never done that before. I actually hear the interpretation coming like a sound. Do you have it, or?

(Jana) No, I'm watching the interpretations.

(Paul) What does the interpretation look like?

(Jana) Well, it came up like grapes that were popping up in different colors, and the interpretation happens when it breaks apart, it flows like a river.

(Paul) Oh, that's—you're very strange.

(Jana) I figure that when we go home (meaning heaven) all of our senses will work together at the same time.

(Paul) That's right. OK, so someone here or online can get the interpretation. Does a tongue realign something? It's a sound, so it could realign something. This is the first time I have heard a tongue interpretation as a sound. This is brand new. I'll have to add this to the list of things I hear. For me, it's new discernment of an interpretation. It's funny; it's like the sound is out there but we just need an antenna to pick it up.

(Jana) It's flowing—like a rainbow river.

Meanwhile, an online webinar participant had shared an anointed interpretation of the tongue, "There's a time coming when all the released souls will be part of the releasing of revival in their area, and will bring the fire to other places to release revival."

It's interesting to note that the interpretation of a tongue may also be musical, as happened during a webinar in 2015, as Jana sang:

You are here Lord
You are holy
We are standing in Your glory

In a discernment session, Paul may ask the participants to pray silently in tongues, taking note of where they feel it happening in/on their heads. Then he will tell them to contrast that feeling with the lack of sensation while simply thinking about an everyday concern such as where to go for dinner, which is an action of the frontal lobe. By paying attention, we can discern where the tongue is occurring in our minds. Paul feels it toward the back of his head, and mine is about halfway back, as if buried right in the center of the top of my brain. Try it yourself, and see what you discern.

We have noticed that when a tongue of fire is present, we may receive clear revelation in just a few moments about something we've been trying to figure out for years.

> *Then there appeared to them divided tongues, as of fire, and one sat upon each of them.*[3]

Paul shares his own experience:

> In the past we've have been taught that we need to pray in tongues for one or two hours a day, but now I may feel a tongue while watching TV, and all of a sudden I speak in tongues. The tongue disappears and I go back to watching TV, but I have noticed that something then happens. This happened just two days ago, and the tongue lasted for quite awhile as I was driving to the pharmacy. Suddenly an idea dropped into my head; it is a book idea, and it wasn't just a thought but was a full-blown outline. I wrote it down, realizing it was the result of the tongue.

Our spiritual gift of tongues is an amazing weapon against the enemy. In fact, the tongues of men were originally scrambled because of evil intent:

> *They said, "Come, let us build ourselves a city, and a tower whose top is in the heavens; let us make a name for ourselves, lest we be scattered abroad over the face of the whole earth."*[4]

This is the epitome of evil. Some translations say 'heaven', but in Hebrew it is 'heavens'. Nimrod purposed to go into the dimensional spaces, and his Tower of Babel is at the origin of the confusion of tongues. 'Babel' means the 'Gate of God', and the city received its name from the Hebrew word *balal*, meaning to jumble.[5] It actually means a gate into the god, or a gate that goes into the dimensions, which was Nimrod's purpose—this is about the grid.[6] The *Encyclopedia Britannica* says that the root of astrology goes back to the tower of Babel, where God said it was so dangerous that if all men could agree with one language nothing would be able to stop their power of unity. With that in mind, isn't the following incident a revelatory rub-it-in-the-enemy's-face discernment?

> In a meeting a lady discerned the interpretation of a tongue in front of her. She saw a line on the left side of her body, which looked like a horizontal line with fire on it. Paul followed the line and realized that it went through a door and a gate—so, off into a dimension.

Isn't it also a blessing that a tongue is a private gift between God and His kids, one on which the enemy cannot eavesdrop? Once again, we see evidence of God using for good that which the enemy would love to corrupt.

> *For he who speaks in a tongue does not speak to men but to God, for no one understands him; however, in the spirit he speaks mysteries.*[7]

I often notice that when I'm shopping I will suddenly find myself quietly praying in tongues as I move through a store. My sense is that these may be tongues of protection against evil entities that have a right to be there. At other times, such an unexpected tongue is obviously one of intercession. Once I was walking down a street with my husband when an urgent-but-quiet tongue began out of the blue. What was this about? I asked my husband if he had a sense of anything and he didn't, but within moments he tripped as his foot caught in an unseen pothole and he fell to his knees, ruining a brand new pair of jeans and scratching up an expensive new wedding ring that was part of a re-commitment we had recently made to each other. My husband reported that it felt like he'd been pushed, but there was nobody visible behind him, and we both realized my tongue had been intercession for protection, and that the enemy was quite upset about our marriage covenant. What might have happened otherwise? Only God knows, but we were certain the results could easily have been much, much worse.

Regardless of the manner in which a tongue is delivered, the gift is evidence of the Presence and Power of God, and is meant for the benefit of the Body of Christ.

> How is it then, brethren? Whenever you come together, each of you has a psalm, has a teaching, has a tongue, has a revelation, has an interpretation. Let all things be done for edification.[8]

CHAPTER FIVE

Power for Living, Power for Dying

Life is tough. If it's not one stressful thing, it's another: not enough money and too many bills, illnesses, dysfunctional relationships, unemployment, loneliness, uncertainty, death, fear of this, that and whatever, and the list goes on. Jesus was clear that in this life we would have trouble:

> *These things I have spoken to you, that in Me you may have peace. In the world you will have tribulation; but be of good cheer, I have overcome the world.* [1]

The good news is that He gives us all we need to endure, persevere, and overcome. He equips us with His armor,[2] and enables us with promises that reflect the Power in which we can rest here on earth, the Power of God that is only available through the Holy Spirit.

> *For I am sure that neither death nor life, nor angels nor rulers, nor things present nor things to come, nor powers, nor height nor depth, nor anything else in all creation, will be able to separate us from the love of God in Christ Jesus our Lord.* [3]

34

Every mature believer has a story to tell about God's faithfulness during his or her own personal trials. For me (Barbara), illness played a big part in God growing me up, proving His sufficiency time and again through life-threatening and/or simply painful ailments. During those traumatic moments, I was always comforted by His truth:

> *Finally, my brethren, be strong in the Lord and in the power of His might. Put on the whole armor of God, that you may be able to stand against the wiles of the devil. For we do not wrestle against flesh and blood, but against principalities, against powers, against the rulers of the darkness of this age, against spiritual hosts of wickedness in the heavenly places. Therefore take up the whole armor of God, that you may be able to withstand in the evil day, and having done all, to stand.[4]*

In fact, it is because of this truth about His Power, that my ministry is named *Standing in Faith,* and my book that grew out of the year I battled breast cancer is *I'm Still Standing.* It is His Power on earth as it is in heaven that enables me, *having done all, to stand.*

Recently, the Lord impressed me to start going back through old handwritten journals to create a searchable database of those entries. Time and again I would read a desperate prayer for help, amazed in retrospect how it could've been such a big deal at the time because in each situation He proved so faithful. In an entry from September 2008, when I was the primary caregiver for my parents, it's clear that I was overwhelmed. I'd just been outside listening to my Dad (who had dementia and was practically blind and deaf) pour out his fear, and had come into the bedroom to steal a few quiet moments, when I wrote, "What to do, Lord?" And before the question was completely written, I heard, "Trust Me." So I will, one day at a time, waiting for You to show us what to do.

Two simple words, "Trust Me," unlocked the Power of God's sufficiency over the next six months, trying though they were. During that time, I relocated my parents to live near me, rented out their house, orchestrated more doctor's appointments than I can count, supported my parents through Mom's cancer surgery that was closely followed by a broken hip, found out Dad had terminal cancer, and finally enjoyed an amazing 5-week-long family reunion as kids and cousins came from far and wide to see Papa and Grandma in their shared room in a nursing home. That hospital room was a finely orchestrated gift from God that allowed them to be cared for by someone other than their kids while enjoying the most peaceful time they'd had together in years. It was a wonderful respite before Dad joyfully went home to his first love, Jesus. Though I've witnessed many deaths as a hospice nurse, my dad's faith and joy was unlike anything I'd ever seen, and it displayed God's Power at work:

> *He brought them out of darkness and the shadow of death, And broke their chains in pieces… He calms the storm, So that its waves are still. Then they are glad because they are quiet; So He guides them to their desired haven.*[5]

Throughout that difficult time God did all things well; so one would think that I'd learned to always trust Him, but fast-forward about 5 ½ years to the time when my mom was dying. Having traveled to New Mexico where she was living with my sister, I was stressing out about whether to stay longer or to go home to California for awhile because Mom was up and down like a yo-yo and I didn't know how long she'd stick around. I was definitely not in His rest, but then, in the middle of the night, I heard those same two words, "Trust me." Once again, I said, "Yes, Lord." (I didn't even recall it was the same thing He'd said in 2008 until I saw it in my old journal.) The next day, sitting at Mom's bedside, I heard, "This is My gift to you." OK, that sounded really good, but what did it mean?

First, a little background. My sweet mother was a dyed-in-the-wool Southern Baptist and I learned long ago not to talk about such things as deliverance, speaking in tongues, dream interpretation, or other 'charismatic' manifestations of God's Power; not because I was afraid of what she'd think, but because when I spoke of such things she'd worry that her daughter had gone off the deep end into the New Age. It didn't matter that she'd once had her own personal visitation from Jesus, not to mention several indisputable angelic encounters under her belt—that was different as far as she was concerned. Also, having been her primary caregiver for five years before she moved to my sister's home, I had often prayed that the Lord would give me a way to remember her when she was gone that didn't focus on me in a parental role telling her what she could and couldn't do. I had no clue of how He could ever make that happen and, to be honest, didn't really expect much of an answer. Oh, me of little faith!

The following email I sent to Paul is just a small taste of the miraculous Power of God at work in my family during the last week of Mom's time with us:

> One thing is for sure, these last days with Mom are out of every box I've ever seen!
>
> On Tuesday she was so agitated I had to give her a ton of meds to try to relax and make her comfortable, but it didn't even touch her except to calm her down just enough to speak coherently. She was so upset that I encouraged her to start telling Jesus about all of the things she was seeing and she went through an amazing deliverance. First, she saw herself in a hole with fire all around, so I asked the Lord to take every part of her out of any ungodly depths and any other dimensions and bring it back to her through His blood. There was an immediate noticeable change, but she was still seeing a lot of stuff. As she described her visions, I realized it was all in 'dream-speak', and we prayed through each thing as it occurred. Eventually, she started talking nonstop to Jesus and I couldn't understand everything she was saying, but fortunately He could! We reached a point where I really thought He might take her right then, so I had Chelsie (my niece) call her mom to come home and Dara (my sister) came blazing in about 30 minutes later. Apparently

she'd driven 90 miles an hour with all of her emergency lights flashing (she drives a county truck for work that has lights on top, just like a police car). Anyway, by the time Dara got here Mom was glowing—her previously dull-and-dead-looking brown eyes were wide and bright, and she was soooo happy. Over the next few hours, the Lord treated us to one choice moment after another, including her checking to make sure every one of us was saved. Mom was an evangelist at heart, and as we told her she'd led each of us to the Lord as a child she would happily exclaim, "I did? I did? Wow!" Finally, my very staid Southern Baptist mother threw her hands up in the air and insisted that we all do the same, and not just a little bit either for she kept saying, "Get those hands up—higher, higher! We've got to praise the Lord!" So we had church, and she turned into a charismatic right before our eyes. Seemingly awestruck, she asked us at one point if we'd ever realized that the Holy Spirit is just like Jesus and you can talk to Him. At one point I mentioned something about living water and she exclaimed, pointing to the corner of her bedroom, "Well of course! The fountain is right there!" She also reported seeing angels all around. The glory was thick! She finally tired out and went back to sleep, only to awaken a few hours later not knowing who we were, but she felt good and was smiling and jolly, wanting to know who we were and where we were born. As we started filling in the details, she'd get a look of wonder on her face and laugh and exclaim, "Really?" Eventually she got tired again and I thought she was going to sleep so I headed off to bed, but Dara came for me in just a few minutes because Mom was having another stroke. I medicated her again and wondered if she'd make it through the night. Amazingly enough, she did.

So we get to yesterday, and on it went as she reported seeing people who were standing there smiling at her—one was a favorite aunt, and another was Dara's first husband and father of her first three kids. Then she described a huge celebration, complete with balloons and banners. I asked who the party was for, thinking she'd say it was a welcome-home party for her, but she totally surprised me when she said, "It's for all of the people who were saved today, and I'm going!" [6] She saw a big man walking around the house and then coming to stand at the foot of her bed, so Dara suggested it might be her guardian angel, but she insisted it wasn't because he was standing next to her guardian angel. Turns out it was Jesus, but she couldn't go with Him yet because she had to wait for Him to open the gate, which was still closed. (Please understand that she knew absolutely nothing about spiritual gates!)

So, here the story takes another turn. I'd had a bad sinus headache all day that I couldn't shake, so I took my sister's truck and went down to a pharmacy that was only a few blocks away to get a different pain reliever. As I pulled out of the parking lot on the way back, I'd almost completed a left turn but was still right in the middle of the street when I was almost blinded by the oncoming headlights of a car on the other side of the street. Seemingly appearing out of nowhere, it was turning left in the opposite direction. I stopped completely and laid down on the horn, but the guy didn't even hesitate and plowed into me headfirst, really messing up the front of both vehicles. Long story short, it was a God-ordained divine appointment. The driver turned out to be the pastor of the church on that corner, and when I blew the horn he'd looked the opposite way but didn't stop because he was confused about what was going on. I called Dara, who came down right away, and we ended up standing there, praying together while we waited for the police to come. The end result is that she invited him home to pray for Mom, and he was glad to come.

The pastor started out reading some scriptures and she

really seemed to like it. It was kind of funny though, because on the one hand he was trying to make sure she knew the Lord, while on the other she was busy explaining the gospel to him. He finally grinned and said, "Well, I guess there's no doubt that's taken care of!" I knew I was supposed to invite him to take part in her funeral because she hasn't found a church she liked since moving to New Mexico. With no local pastor, we'd previously decided I was going to do the service. He was thrilled, and said he was really blessed by this whole encounter, adding that he'd really needed this. Then he hung around and visited with us for about an hour, and it turned out he's played against my sister on an opposing softball team and they have mutual friends. As if that wasn't enough, God wasn't finished yet, and he also offered the use of his church so we don't have to use the funeral home. Had we planned it, we couldn't have found a better location or facility—there is literally no church in Las Cruces that is any closer.

Oh, and you're going to love this. After talking to Ross (my brother) on the phone with a daily update, he hung up and told the Lord he wanted everything to be done in His timing. Then he "happened" to look down at his odometer, which read 77.7. As you say Paul, you just can't make this stuff up!!!

Believe me when I say the above account is just a taste of the gracious outpouring of God's Spirit; an outpouring that was nothing less than multiple manifestations of His Power as He blessed my mom and my family beyond belief, transforming a time of loss and grief into a celebration of Jesus' victory over death, and answering my desperate prayer for a pleasant way to remember my mother. It was indeed His gift to me.

Be anxious for nothing, but in everything by prayer and supplication, with thanksgiving, let your requests be made known to God; and the peace of God, which surpasses all understanding, will guard your hearts and minds through Christ Jesus.[7]

What can be more relevant to a discussion of God's Power on earth as it is in heaven than His power over death? The moment of death, that instant in time when we put off the limitations of the physical realm, is not the terrible threat to a Christian that it is for one who hasn't accepted Jesus. Two of the biggest blessings of my entire life have been the privilege of being there to observe God at work in the magnificent home-goings of each of my parents.

Precious in the sight of the Lord is the death of His saints.[8]

So when this corruptible has put on incorruption, and this mortal has put on immortality, then shall be brought to pass the saying that is written: "Death is swallowed up in victory. O Death, where is your sting? O Hades, where is your victory?[9]

Certainly, the death of someone we love is accompanied by grief and loss, and our own approaching death may be a fearsome prospect for one reason or another, but when God's Power over death is realized on earth, we are much better equipped to handle it and we can be comforted by His promises.

CHAPTER SIX

Unfolding Revelation of God's Power

It was September 2015, and *Exploring Heavenly Places, Power in the Heavenly Places* was almost complete, but we were far from finished writing about Power. The month was also the intersection of many other significant events, not the least of which was the fourteenth anniversary of the 9/11 terrorist attack. Rosh Hashanah (Jewish New Year) fell on September 13th, or Elul 29 on the Hebrew calendar. It marked the end of a Shemitah year and was closely followed by Yom Kippur (Day of Atonement), which began the 70th Year of Jubilee.[1] Mix in the occurrence of the fourth blood moon of a rare tetrad of lunar eclipses on the 28th,[2] and a cacophony of prophetic voices filled the air regarding end-times events. Additionally, September brought other religious and historic events such as the Muslim Feast of Sacrifice and pilgrimage to Mecca (Hajj), the Pope's address to the U.S. Congress and the U.N General assembly, CERN (Switzerland) firing at full power, and a meeting of the French Prime Minister and John Kerry over climate change, to name just a few.[3]

In the midst of all of this, the Lord was leading me (Barbara) to travel to Maple Grove, MN to attend a series of meetings that Paul had scheduled for September 11-13th. He hadn't realized the significance of the dates when he set up the meetings but now, as the time for our departure from Southern CA drew near, the increasing volume of gloomy prophetic warnings and governmental travel advisories made us wonder if we should just stay home. Paul even heard a prediction that anyone traveling on 9/11 wouldn't be able to fly home on 9/12. As we pondered and prayed, we left the decision in the Lord's very capable hands and asked Him to close the doors and make it clear if the conference should be canceled. He didn't, and we went. The peace and rest we enjoyed in the midst of such a decision is, in itself, evidence of God's Power on earth as it is in heaven.

> *Come to Me, all you who labor and are heavy laden, and I will give you rest. Take My yoke upon you and learn from Me, for I am gentle and lowly in heart, and you will find rest for your souls. For My yoke is easy and My burden is light.[4]*

As the Maple Grove meetings began, the presence of the Lord was immediately evident, and it quickly became apparent that this was going to be an incredible weekend. By the time it was over, much of the content of this book (plus more) had been explored, including breakthrough, the golden pipes, tongues of angels, windows and branches. On Sunday, September 13th, which was also Rosh Hashanah, a re-appearance of the Rainbow Angel[5] had me wondering how to fit more into *Volume 4*, but we decided to expand as necessary in this book.

To review, a rainbow is a representation of God's covenant promises to man, as first manifested in Genesis 9:17:

> *And God said to Noah, "This is the sign of the covenant which I have established between Me and all flesh that is on the earth."*

Consider the importance of the following account that seers reported from Minnesota on September 13th, Rosh Hashanah, when a rainbow angel manifested. The angel, appearing with keys to shut ungodly places of death, was smiling and his face was extremely bright, beaming with life and energy. He brought a scroll, which Anthony Huselbus[6] read, prefacing it with his sense of holy fear, which he described as a deep reverence combined with a righteous fear of the Lord, perhaps similar to the feelings expressed by biblical characters when they were confronted with an angel bearing a message from God:

> The Lord says, "I'm here today with my angel to speak to you, and I'm announcing a new covenant of life with you. You've heard it said that the covenant with America is broken but I tell you, it is not. You've heard it said that Israel and America will be broken but I tell you they will not. My covenant with the blood of the patriots and saints in this nation is still in their blood and in my blood. The blood of Israel and the blood of America are mixed together. I'm announcing today that I'm renewing and realigning the covenant to all those who enter in and reaffirm my covenant through Christ the Holy One. I will reaffirm new life to this nation, and to you in this room. You are the bearers of my covenant. I announce to you, even as the generations in Numbers, even as new generations have the chance to walk in My covenant, you have the chance today to walk in and to be holders and bearers of a continual and renewed covenant with this nation and all of my people in the earth. I'm sending my angel to remind you that my covenant stands forever for those that enter in. I'm sending new life into your bones. The curse of death will not stand in America. There is more to be revealed. I am asking you to stand to your feet and walk into the presence of my covenant and new life."

Anthony observed that the angel was really joyous and continued, "This is a new covenant and a new day. The Garden of Eden is still there. He's destroying this place of death. The angel has keys. We need to ask for the keys to shut our place of death. This tomb is symbolic. The enemy has tried to put a tomb on America. It needs to be destroyed."

In the ongoing discussion a participant reminded us:

When the rainbow was put on the White House and they announced the breaking of the marriage covenant, the enemy tried to steal the marriage covenant. He won't get away with that. It's God's sign.

Someone else mentioned a rainbow had appeared over Ground Zero two days earlier on 9/11, the first day of the conference, and we were reminded of Revelation 10:5-7:

The angel whom I saw standing on the sea and on the land raised up his hand to heaven and swore by Him who lives forever and ever, who created heaven and the things that are in it, the earth and the things that are in it, and the sea and the things that are in it, that there should be delay no longer, but in the days of the sounding of the seventh angel, when he is about to sound, the mystery of God would be finished, as He declared to His servants the prophets.

Another participant recalled a dream that had been shared the night before about an old woman who initially seemed frumpy and irrelevant, but who appeared later as a stunning, regal beauty, just like the Bride. In the dream she was wearing a shawl with a rainbow, and now we each seemed to be wearing one. On the shawl was an emblem, which Anthony saw in Hebrew and translated:

I give to those who find it and choose it. I give the Tree of Life in the Garden of Eden to those who choose it. My words and spirit and they are life. I am opening up doors that have never been open before; even in America I am opening doors with the covenant of America and Israel. They were never open until this year, and I will reveal the mysteries that have been hidden for the ages to those who will seek life and will hold fast to my covenant.

Paul then continued:

Lord, we choose to take the key; we choose in unity to shut this place of death. Lord, we choose to open the place of life.

The angel is here to renew the covenant of life. Have faith in the covenant of life, rejecting the covenant of death.[7]

We're approaching Rosh Hashanah, and it's already Rosh Hashanah in Israel, 5776, the Year of the Hammer.

What better way to begin a new year with the Lord than to embrace His everlasting covenant promises as revealed by a rainbow angel?

For the mountains shall depart
And the hills be removed,
But My kindness shall not depart from you,
Nor shall My covenant of peace be removed,"
Says the Lord, who has mercy on you...
This is the heritage of the servants of the Lord,
And their righteousness is from Me,"
Says the Lord.[8]

CHAPTER SEVEN

Puzzling Pieces of Revelation

Sometimes it's necessary to wait a long time to discover what we need to understand. Until that 'ah-ha' moment, it seems as if we are floundering in a sea of information that does not make any sense. But then, at a pivotal moment, the Wisdom of the Lord breaks through the morass of human thinking, and suddenly we begin to comprehend what previously was not at all clear. It is not easy to be patient in the process, and faith is essential while waiting until the matter is fully revealed. Along the journey, there are many threads that are given, which somehow are eventually woven by the Lord into a beautiful garment. One such thread began on September 15, 2005, with words I (Paul) did not understand and concepts that were far beyond my ability to comprehend. I did realize that the ultimate goal is salvation of the lost; an outpouring of healing, and complete sense of freedom in Christ; but the journey has taken a long time. Perhaps, we are now beginning to see what was not seen before.

For many years, it has been my contention that the Lord does want to see us healed, and the issue is not with Him but with us. As a pastor, I became aware that we have stifled the Holy Spirit and His gifts by not listening to Him, and we have not given permission for the gifts to be released among His people so the revelation could be released that would result in healing. Unfortunately, many of us have not only failed to release the gifting in others, but have also taught that the gifts were not even to be used. We cannot know the amount of unknown pain and hardship that has resulted from such attitudes within the church and among unbelievers.

Following is an account of my journey in trying to be obedient to the words of the Lord and seeking to understand the mysteries of the Kingdom of God so that we can walk in total health and freedom. As I mention often, this journey is traveled with others as we walk in unity, exercising our gifts according to the workings of the Holy Spirit. I must warn you that this is not a simplistic and easy-to-understand journey. Our wonderful Heavenly Father has created a complex world, and I am reminded of the words of Hebrews 5:11, which speak of Melchizedek and the gift of discernment:

> *... of whom [Melchizedek] we have much to say, and hard to explain, since you have become dull of hearing.*

On September 15, 2005, Mimi Lowe[1] received this word from an angelic messenger:

> There's a demonic council going on in the spirit realm...It's plotting and planning. They're huddled together. Territorial spirits have landed. There's a strategy in there. You've got to send in your forces to go in there to grab the blue prints. You need more warfare to retrieve those blue prints. You can go in there in the Spirit, but you have to protect yourself. They're plotting for your demise, but you will prevail.
>
> There's another aspect you have not known. They're connectors. They need to be uncovered. You've got to

find them and dismantle them. When it's time, we will direct you and you can go in there.

The second thread appeared one year later on August 6, 2006 when Jana Green, Dale Shannon[2] and I were together, and the presence of the Lord came upon us. The Lord began speaking through Jana and Dale:

(Dale) I will establish my truth. I will establish my righteousness. This is the grand finale. This is the war of all ages. The release of the warriors is for the war of all wars. Expansion is coming. Don't limit what God intends to do. Raise up the youth to fly higher...They will soar higher. Training for the youth. They need to be raised up. That is what Aslan's Place is to do...I am raising up a new generation of fearless warriors, so teach my children.

(Jana) It's a trumpet call going forth. It's a gathering and releasing. Do not tarry. Take the vision and run with it. It's a mandate, to teach the youth. You've cried forth for the little ones. Your joy will be complete. The harvest is coming. Divine wisdom is being released in little ones not by natural parents. Don't limit Him to man's understanding. Let them run. Release them. This is my move. This is not random...this is my move...my outpouring! Connectors. Releasing Connectors. Vector field[3] momentum will be poured out on all the earth.

We had never heard the term, 'vector field', before. What did this mean? It became apparent that somehow connectors and vector fields were tied together.

One year later, Dale Shannon received another prophetic word for our puzzle, and then continued to get even more words into 2009:

(August 17, 2007 at Aslan's Place) Living stones, established [and knit together] one upon another. One body. Connections. You are connected to Me first, then to one another. Break off evil connections. Rest in Me. It is the force field, the vector force field that is spinning. Line upon line [with] My force connecting the line...new revelation. It is by My power, by My force, that all things are connected together. Without me you can do nothing. Yield to My power and to My force and I will increase My power within you. This is the time I have waited for from the beginning to pour out my power, my force...Step into...My dimensions.

(August 4, 2008, in Hawaii) Vector force field; lines of communication; cut the wires; decontaminate the connectors. For My people shall be a holy people. They shall be one as We are...this is a key to unlocking the mysteries of the kingdom: one spirit, one body, one flesh. Father, Son, Holy Spirit. Clean the highways of holiness. Frequencies, sounds, vibrations, these are connectors...as you tune in to Me and not the earth you will vibrate with Me. Cleanse the force field of ungodly vibrations. You must resonate with My frequencies, sounds, and vibrations. As you are filled with My glory, the force field will change. Matter changes. You are connected to Me, and I can move you into My realm...Listen to the sounds of My kingdom...There's a new sound, a new vibration, a new groan. The sons of man are being revealed for such a time as this. As the earth groans, a new sound is produced—My sound. Sheaves of disobedience will be burnt. Only what I have created in My glory will remain through the fire of purification. You must be disconnected from the land, the earth and be connected to My kingdom, My realm. Faster than you think, matter will be changed in a twinkling of an eye. Whose are you? Are you connected to the world or to Me? Let go of ungodly connections that I have not ordained. Tune into My Spirit, My frequency. You will hear My voice and the sounds of My kingdom. Rejoice, for the hour is come for the sons of man to be revealed. One kingdom, one spirit, one voice, one sound in Me, for I have ordained it to be.

Listen to what the Spirit is saying. Let go of your divisions and your kingdom building. It's in the tree. It's in the source. Disconnect from the tree of knowledge of good and evil and connect to the tree of life. Disconnect from deadness and connect to life. You will vibrate with my heartbeat...My kingdom vibrates with Me. Contamination began with connecting to the tree of knowledge of good and evil. Disconnect from the tree of knowledge and connect to the tree of life. You will pulsate with my kingdom. In Me there is life, newness, oneness, and unity.

(March 13, 2009) They're all connected—the sounds, lights, colors, frequencies, connections, living stones, living colors, and living lights—it's all in My breath. There are thrones at the gates, unholy, unholy 8s at the gates. I establish My living stones at the gates of the New Jerusalem. Living stones are at the gates of My city, but in man's city they are unholy thrones based on structures of 8s. The thrones are at the gates. Tear down the thrones...take down the gates, the ungodly gates, and My people are set free to come into my city, the New Jerusalem. Vibrant stones, living stones will establish the New Jerusalem, one up on another in My spirit, My living Spirit. These stones will not be torn down. Eternal stones, living stones; they will magnify My name for all eternity. There is life, sound, vibration, praise, and worship in the stones. These are the godly stones. This is New Jerusalem built on the godly stones of colors, sounds, vibrations, frequencies and lights—energy, electromagnetic energy, force fields, and vector force fields. (Paul confirms that the energy is strong) Contamination, they are contaminated. There's a shaft of light. Come up higher.

(March 20, 2009) The mark of the beast is the ungodly branding, ungodly fire, marked for and stolen from future generations. It is an ungodly cord from the past to the future and it is still connected. It is stealing life, blood. Ungodly covenants were made for the worship of the dragon, sealed with a branding of the future generations…It is stealing life, sucking life and energy. These are the jewels that the enemy has stolen. These are the parts of the DNA; the parts of the DNA are the jewels. Crack the DNA code…I am giving you a key to crack the code…This is the mystery of Babylon…Numbers, vibrations, colors, frequencies are all parts of the code that was written. This is the enemy's plan to take back what he lost when he was cast down, to steal and rob from the generations. He knew what he lost so he defiled the sound, the vibrations, light, frequencies, and worship. It is a symphony of defilement. This is the ungodly covering; it is in the sound, light, vibration; an ungodly covering, it comes and goes and hides. Unravel; unravel the covering. Unravel the dark gauze, the ungodly vibrations and sounds. No more will this come against My children…Look to the sound, light, and vibrations…There was trading that was done, the souls of man for power, but they will be reversed. It is in the numbers. The base of 2, 8, 4; it is the quadrants. That is where there's a shifting from one quadrant to another. Rubik's cubes, the shifting of like Rubik's cubes. Keep shifting the combination locks. Going from one quadrant to another; dimensional shift; find the quadrants, the cube, the piece. Bring it back, bring it back—the necessary piece in the quadrants. The guardian is at the gate, but I give you the key. Unlock the gate. Take the piece, like a piece of the Rubik's cube. The guardian is like a dragon, guarding the gate of the cave. The order has been given from the Lord, the Most High. The guardian must give up. Do not be afraid. Go into the cave and get the key. It is a white stone; it is a stone of identity.

At this point, Dale was aware that she was holding a piece of a Rubik's cube. Returning after a break, Dale reported that the cube piece had turned into a chess king piece. Somehow, the king piece was the key. In chess, the goal is to take out the king, with the term 'checkmate' coming from a Persian word that means 'to kill the king'. In the ancient world, when the lunar and solar calendars came into alignment once every eight years, the king would be sacrificed in the spring. Similarly, the war of the ages is meant to kill the King of Kings, but what did this word mean? It would be a long time until we finally understood. Meanwhile, the revelation continued unfolding a bit at a time:

(August 10, 2009) Release the convoys; release the carriers, the transports. Buckets of revelation are being released. Train the receptors of your beings…there is so much I want to give you, but are you ready to receive? You desire, but are you ready?

Purify your hearts…cleanse, purify…There is a pure stream…Take away the mixture, the defilement. For My people will be a holy people and you will desire Me alone and you will be built up. You will honor Me alone, not man, not self.

Purify your desires. You put self on the throne for too long. A light force is coming…a vector force, a field of revelation. The stars are singing. Rejoice, rejoice, because you are becoming one with Me—one heart, one spirit, one mind, one goal. Are you ready to be joined with Me, with my heart? Unity of the spirit, unity of the mind, unity of the heart; single focus…remove the distractions.

Love [and] honor one another. Take away the condemnation, the accusation; the religious spirit…for My people will be a people that love, a people that I can trust with the new revelation that is coming.

The starry hosts are rejoicing and they come in unity with you to teach you to honor one another, to love one another. They will be your teachers. I want to take you out of your plastic world…that has confined you. I want to take you out of the depths of confinement and raise you up to a place of contentment, rejoicing, pleasure, a place of overcoming.

You will occupy the land that I give you [and] take [it] back…you will become overcomers and will take back that which has been taken and stolen from you.

Will you come up higher to the place of revelation, the place of rejoicing, the place of worship? Because it is about Me, not about you. I have longed for you. I wooed you, and called you, and longed for you.

It is living in the blood; there is life in the blood; cleanse, purify the blood and there will be wholeness. Restore the element to wholeness. Layer upon layer, stone upon stone. I'm giving you keys to wholeness, health, wealth, pleasures, and joy.

Why are you downcast? I call you out. You do not need to be under. There is a force, a spring that will push you free, release you, and cause you to fly higher and higher to the heavenly realms [where] there is safety. There is joy, peace, hope and pleasure—joy that you've never known. I call you out of the depths.

Hear My voice, My cry. Follow the sound…there's treasure…the hidden treasure. The hidden treasure will be exposed to build My kingdom. I release these treasures of darkness to build My kingdom. Will you build My kingdom with the gifts, the callings, the wealth? Will you build My treasures? Will you build My kingdom? Stone upon stone, layer upon layer, stone upon stone, higher and higher.

You are seated with Me in the heavenly realms, and I give you keys this day to unlock, uncover, underneath and to come up higher. The key is in the sound…it's in the light; it's in the rays; it's in the force field. My children, I give you these keys because the day is coming; confusion, chaos, but you will be stable if you hold onto the keys.

There are so many that are in the place of captivity that the Lord wants to bring out. Autism is going to be exposed; healings, multiple healings; I will heal the mind, the brain; the keys are in the elements…study the elements…appropriate them. This is part of your healing.

This is a part of your test too. Study hard; tests are coming; get ready; the answers are here; the answers are clear. You must receive and study; you must be a wise Berean…you are approved…don't doubt, don't shrink back, and don't hesitate. This is what you've desired. You just didn't know it. This is what you've been calling out for; crying out for, and I've heard your cries in the secret season.

I will fill your cups to overflowing; manna, fresh manna; not stale, not broken, but fresh, and you will participate with Me. I will close many doors. I will open many doors; new dimensions, new places, new seasons, new times, with the time capsule taking you forwards, backwards.

Healing, healing, healing, that which you thought could never be healed. You thought you were stuck. Have I not told you? With Me all things are possible if you believe. Will you trust? Will you believe? I have much to show you, much to tell you.

Remove doubt; remove confusion, hopelessness and hope deferred. I give you new hope…faith. Step into the faith realm…it is for My pleasure that I give you good gifts. It is for My pleasure.

By this point, if you have not given up, you are undoubtedly wondering what this has to do with anything! Nine years into this revelation, I was too! Would I ever be able to make sense of what the Lord was telling us? Yes, and our journey continues...

CHAPTER EIGHT

The Missing Piece

Here we were in April 2014, with lots of puzzle pieces that didn't seem to fit together, when Persis Tiner[1] received a rhyme from the Lord that confused us even further:

> It's under the sea
> It's under the sea
> You are going
> You are going
> And it is with me
> The enemy won't like it
> He'll try to intervene
> But I have you covered
> And I have a plan
> To bring revelation and knowledge
> To uncover new gateways
> To explore rich new spheres
> Of my vastness
> Of my treasures

> I have hidden 'till now
> So fasten your seat belts
> Expect lots of fun
> As you help to implode
> What the enemy has done

We had no comprehension of what Persis' word meant at the time, but then the Lord surprised us in September 2014, during an *Exploring Heavenly Places* seminar in Roseburg, Oregon. It was as if we had been viewing life with binoculars that were out of focus and suddenly a friend came along, heard our complaints of not making sense of what we were seeing, and said, "Let me put this into focus for you." With an adjustment that we were not even aware of, we could now see clearly. It was another ah-ha moment.

As I (Paul) was teaching, we became aware of Gabriel's presence, and then he started flying with us in the heavenly places, traveling slowly into the depth, and then into the lower parts of the depth. We were aware of fallen stars there, and the Lord revealed that much had happened at the origin of our spirit and soul, and there were issues to be addressed that would result in a change of position for us.

I was reminded of a dream I had in 2003 in which I was in Nevada, traveling on a train far out into the desert to nowhere, and I had to get back to a city called Delta[2] that was on the border of California and Nevada. I was on the train, but I could not get back because there was a canyon on the right side and no matter what I would do, I couldn't cross over it to return to Delta. At the first stop, I found myself at a wonderful hotel surrounded by beautiful scenery, but the train wasn't going back so I was stuck and frustrated, in spite of the hotel's beauty. I also noticed that the train was filled with lots of baggage, which I believe represented all my issues from the past. At the next stop, I saw a small, dilapidated trailer in a desert scene, with several individuals sitting around a small fire. It looked like a gypsy camp, and spoke to me of poverty. I was now even further out into the desert, literally nowhere. I thought, "How am I ever going to get back to Delta?"

During the following night I woke up and heard, "XYZ-axis,"[3] so that day I called a friend who is a knowledgeable about math. I told him about my dream and what I'd heard and asked, "How do I get back to Delta, and what does XYZ-axis have to do with all of this?" Somehow I knew that the train was on the Z-axis, and Delta was on the Y-axis, but how could I get there? I was informed that on a XYZ-axis, the point where the three come together is called the origin, and you have to go back to the origin to get to Delta.

For years, I pondered this dream. Then in 2012, our daughter Corrie and her family moved to Las Vegas, and my son-in-law started working at a solar power plant. I had not connected their move with my dream until the following year when we stayed at a hotel at Lake Las Vegas. It was the hotel from my dream! By January 2014, we were noticing a dramatic change at Aslan's Place, which has intensified in 2015. During this period, the Lord had been continually teaching us how to go further and further back to our origin, moving us into ever increasing blessings in the process.

Finally, in 2014, nine years since the revelation began, the Lord was giving new direction about how to undo what the enemy has done because of humanity's generational agreement with evil. Gabriel had just taken us to one of the points of the origin, the Lord had revealed that there was a gate that he wanted us to take possession of, and we had business to do—it was now time to deal with an ungodly gate and many ungodly doors.[4] As previously explained, the key to doors and gates is to ask the Lord to close and seal all ungodly open doors and to open all righteous doors that should be opened. We may also ask Him for the keys to lock and unlock doors.

We then became aware of the Seven Spirits of God, and the Lord was focusing on the Spirit of Wisdom, and the Lord started speaking about the ungodly trading floor and the chessboard.[5] Where was this going now? At times, I felt as if adrift on the ocean, completely lost. However, we continued following the leading of the Lord as He directed each step.

Next, I began discerning the fallen sons of God, especially Moloch. I also discerned Satan and a fallen cherub. Many of us felt fire, and I discerned the fiery stones mentioned in Ezekiel 28:14–18:

> *You were the anointed cherub who covers; I established you; you were on the holy mountain of God; you walked back and forth in the midst of fiery stones. You were perfect in your ways from the day you were created, till iniquity was found in you. By the abundance of your trading you became filled with violence within, And you sinned; Therefore I cast you as a profane thing Out of the mountain of God; And I destroyed you, O covering cherub, From the midst of the fiery stones. Your heart was lifted up because of your beauty; you corrupted your wisdom for the sake of your splendor; I cast you to the ground, I laid you before kings that they might gaze at you. You defiled your sanctuaries by the multitude of your iniquities, by the iniquity of your trading; therefore I brought fire from your midst; It devoured you, And I turned you to ashes upon the earth In the sight of all who saw you.*

The Lord was showing us that, at our physical origin, the physical elements of our body were contaminated because the elemental spirits *(stoicheia)*[6] were contaminated[7] at the Fall. In other words, the original coding on our original design, our original 'operating system', our very core, was defiled at the very beginning, which would result in a corruption of our DNA and RNA.[8]

Tobias Renken, who initially seemed to be climbing a spiritual ladder, began speaking prophetic words (in quotes), followed by his observations of what he was experiencing concurrently:

> "Shaking, shaking." There is a false reflection, like the moon reflecting the sun, but ungodly. We feel the fallen sons of God and the ungodly stars.

> "I am shaking this place, I'm shaking this place, shaking, shaking the earth. Don't you see that? It's the foundation, the foundation. You stand on the foundation and I am shaking, I'm shaking, I'm shaking." Now, Tobias was

walking up stairs of a temple, a huge giant ancient temple, perhaps the original ungodly temple.

"I don't want this temple I am disgusted by it. A breaking has to come. It's time; it's time; it's time for My people. It is time for My people to have freedom in the land. My people have forgotten who I am. It is time to awake out of your sleep. No longer sleeping. The day is coming. Break the old foundation. Break them all open. Break them open. The kingdom is coming. The enemy's kingdom is falling. The enemy's kingdoms are falling across the nations because My kingdom is being established. Before that happens, the enemy's kingdom needs to fall. Can you hear the sound?"

Then the Lord began speaking to us about times and seasons. In the ungodly origin, the lunar calendar that was God's calendar was abandoned for the solar calendar. All of the current months and days have ties to other gods, the fallen sons of God,[9] and we have abandoned God's Kairos time and installed the enemy's Chronos time. The Lord wants to rid mankind of all ungodly times and seasons, which are part of the kingdoms of the enemy.

It was now time to take possession of the gate the Lord had revealed to us. I walked inside the gate with another person, and the Lord revealed a door. At the end of the dimensional corridor there was a pig, an ungodly sacrifice, being roasted on a spit, so we repented for this sin in our family lines. It appears that the enemy may have actually genetically engineered the human genome with pig DNA.

We sensed He was moving us into the heavenly places. Where were we going now? As the Lord moved us along, we could feel Him cleaning out places, but why did we again discern the pig? People in the room were feeling fire on their feet, which was identified as His fiery stream:[10]

A fiery stream issued

And came forth from before Him.
A thousand thousands ministered to Him;
Ten thousand times ten thousand stood before Him.
The court was seated,
And the books were opened.

We asked the Lord to cause His fiery stream to come and deal with this evil and the blasphemous sacrifices. Now the lightnings[11] of the Lord were hitting the evil. A great deliverance took place and lasted for several minutes.

I checked the gate and discerned that the gate was now clean. We understood that this gate was the key to a missing piece. But what was this missing piece?

I had a sense that the conference organizers, Diane Bryant and Sharon Pfeiffer, now had a key to open this gate, and we laughed because their ministry is called Keys to the Kingdom. Sharon inserted the key into the keyhole, and Diane opened the gate. I discerned an open door to the left of us. I walked in and felt nothing, but sensed I was to walk further to the left. Suddenly I knew I was discerning Melchizedek, and remembered the word that Dale Shannon had on March 13, 2009. She had seen the king piece on the chessboard, and it had been isolated from us. Then the revelation struck, and I said:

> Our understanding of the importance of Melchizedek is the missing piece! He, Jesus, as our High Priest, Melchizedek, is the key to the final release of healing. Melchizedek is the King of Righteousness and the King of Peace. He is not dead! Our King has not been killed, as the enemy would like us to believe. Melchizedek has not been removed from the chessboard by the ungodly king. Melchizedek is forever alive as the King of Kings and the Lord of Lords. Melchizedek is the One who trumps all other pieces on the chessboard. He holds all the keys to all the gates and doors in the heavenly places. He is the One who moves throughout all of the heavenly

places. He is the beginning and the end of our understanding of vector force fields. The game is over.

Suddenly others' words made sense as well. On September 8, 2010, Jana Green had received this word from the Lord:

These are in counsel for your sake—for all your sakes. They want to give what's theirs to you so it won't be too late...Expect, discern and believe to seek His face. If your heart is wise, than you make My heart glad, for in My inmost place, what you speak, you can have. It's been given to you, to trade back the DNA. For the order of Melchizedek has made this day. The sound begets light, the creative force. For transference is waiting, transference for the course. Creation itself is groaning, and Zion can't wait. For these standing here have been waiting for the revealing of the sons...Your position was sure, and the covenant was made. Renounce the other covenants for this is the day. It's being written, it's being recorded now. These were the crowns; take what is yours. The government at the gate, what's given in marriage; it's not too late.

A person attending the seminar then said:

I see the cube spinning like a Rubik's cube. Everything is spinning and when you said you felt an energy spot it was like it is missing a piece. Ask the Lord if that is the piece that's trapped. What does this Rubik's cube represent? Life!

I responded:

The Lord says that this is the key to healing, the key to autism. In the vision, the dragon was supervising and protecting that piece. It is too late. The enemy has lost. This is the tipping point.

Remember, in 2010, we had no idea what this all meant; but suddenly it had now become clear. Adam and Eve gave away all the keys to the gates and the doors in the dimensional places. It would take another Adam, the second Adam, to buy back those keys by His death on the cross through His resurrection power.

...that I may know Him and the power of His resurrection...[12]

CHAPTER NINE

Breakthrough

Over the years, I (Paul) have gone on many family vacations. During the early years, we did not have the luxury of a GPS, so I would get out the maps and carefully plot the route to a destination. Maps from the American Automobile Association were very helpful because they noted the amount of time it would usually take to travel between points. I liked this; I liked planning, setting goals, and determining how long it would take to get somewhere. There is a certain security in having this kind of control over a schedule.

As a pastor, I also liked planning in detail for the future, and would often plan one whole year in advance. As a church staff, we then knew exactly where we were going and we thought we knew how to get there. Unfortunately, by doing this there was a tendency to ignore the Lord's direction and the adventure He had for us. I still wonder if we missed the manifold blessings He intended for us to have. How grateful I am to the Lord that He has moved me into a new paradigm.

The shift from my former way of planning into a new mind set has taken many years. What was once a definite routine has now become a surprise-filled adventure. A word that wonderfully expresses this concept is 'serendipity'. Horace Walpole first coined the word in 1754, in a letter he wrote to Horace Mann. He related how the princes in a Persian fairy tale, *The Three Princes of Serendip* (the old name for Sri Lanka), were always making discoveries of things they were not looking for. It was the surprises that gave the thrill to the adventure.

I had a serendipity moment while I was ministering in the greater Houston area in 2014. The worship part of the service was in progress and, sitting on the front row of the church, I was trying to discern the direction of the Lord for the upcoming moments. Aware of the spiritual clouds, I opened my computer to look at my notes. Scanning them, I noticed that I had included Micah 2:13 as a reference. But why? I recognized the verse as one I often use in relation to a talk about the 'breakthrough gate', but could not remember why I had included it in my notes about clouds. Looking at the context, I began reading at Micah 2:6, and came across the word, 'prattler', twice in the passage. I had never seen that word before.

Opening my Bible software to find out what prattler meant, I was stunned. The Hebrew word means 'drip or drop'.[1] In the passage, the Lord is speaking of false prophecy, false words, that are the prattler of the prophets.

My mind raced as I realized that clouds are made up of drops of water,[2] and then I read Micah 2:13:

> *The one who breaks open will come up before them;*
> *They will break out,*
> *Pass through the gate,*
> *And go out by it;*
> *Their king will pass before them,*
> *With the Lord at their head.*

I wondered, "Is there a connection between ungodly spiritual clouds, the negative words spoken against a person,[3] and the key to a breakthrough in one's life?"

I first discerned the breakthrough gate on July 31, 2012. Praying for a pastor and his wife, I felt parallel bars on the top back of my head, and sensed this was a gate. The Lord gave me the word, 'breakthrough'. I had never started a prayer session like this, yet suddenly I felt the deliverance beginning, and could feel the deliverance going through the gate. We felt the Lord say to us, "Baal Perazim, the Lord of the Breakthrough."

I called my friend, Larry Pearson,[4] and shared with him what was happening; and he received this word from the Lord:

> This has been a hidden gate, hidden in the depths. There will be a greater opening to the greater glory, greater authority, greater steps of faith. There's a returning, a returning. It's something about stepping back into what has been said. There's a returning and a yearning of what has been said. I'm bringing a day of understanding of what has been said for this gate is now open. Greater dimensions, a greater weight of glory, signs will follow. Greater amperage. He's turning up the amperage of that vacuum of evil, to vacuum out the evil. There are new ranks of angels coming. My sense is a new key to unlock things. This key is an ability to unlock souls, to unlock treasures, unlock the dreams. The waters of breakthrough, you have unlocked the waters of breakthrough. Breakthrough shall follow you all the rest of your days and the train of your sphere is coming through into the springs and the waters of breakthrough. A new key will make them see. Something about going deeper into the depths. I see a new diving suit to go back into the depths, to go into the deeper depths. New strategies, new systems to dismantle, new treasures to be found; breakthrough has a sound. Breakthrough has a

sound that will unlock the ground, open up the depths. It's a springtime. It's a springtime.

Baal Perazim is mentioned in 2 Samuel 5:20, and is in the context of David taking Jerusalem:

> *So David went to Baal Perazim, and David defeated them there; and he said, "The Lord has broken through my enemies before me, like a breakthrough of water." Therefore he called the name of that place Baal Perazim. And they left their images there, and David and his men carried them away.*

As the prayer session continued, the pastor's wife received this word:

> The Lord is saying to the enemy, "Enough. You have had your time. I have sent a breakthrough angel to bring you into God's plan and he will stay with you to complete what God has for you. He is a door opener. He is releasing the supernatural; releasing wealth as a tool; it is a release of His kingdom in the earth. We will never be able to say we did it our own strength or power. There will be a release of healing gifts.

I was about to have another surprise. A month after the first revelation of the breakthrough gate, Crystal Kain Ross[5] contacted me with a word she had just heard from the Lord. She was not aware of what had happened, so it was a stunning confirmation of what the Lord was speaking to us about the breakthrough gate.

> I received this word for you a little over a week ago. I saw a place in the high heavens. Most of the time what I see up there is blue, beautiful, living and alive. The air is usually pure to breathe, and very fresh. What I saw before me now was utter desolation. Everywhere I looked, the sky above and below was as a dark, barren desert. Nothing was growing. There was no water to be found anywhere. The air was dusty and difficult to

breathe. I asked Lord what this meant. He said, "What you are seeing is a representation of the spiritual state of the majority of mankind upon the Earth. They have sought their own way. They have become their own source. They are as gods unto themselves. They have believed many lies and delusions. These lies have been laid craftily, as a spiders web, (via Hollywood entertainment, and thru other hidden agents), for the last two generations. The state of many is as a barren desert, a literal desolation. Their worldly pleasure seeking and carnal indulgences have brought them to this place. My heart breaks, for they are asleep in the desolation of their own dust[6] wherein they have chosen to make their beds, and lie down with devils. There is a great famine in the Earth. It is both a literal famine of Judgment, and a famine for drinking in My Holy, living words. They have chosen to drink in filth instead of holiness. They love the darkness and are offended by My light. Therefore, once again, I have purposed to send forth torrents of My mercy, for this has become a depraved and desolate generation of self-seekers. This shall be evidenced by the breaking forth of many high-and-holy waters, which have been building up in my spiritual reservoirs all over the earth. For years, I have built many sons and daughters to become spiritual dams and reservoirs of My truth and light. Let the breaking forth of the waters commence! As the waters break out, so the Lord has broken out against His enemies.

It would be another two years before the Lord would draw attention again to the breakthrough gate. We were in Kaneohe, Hawaii, when Jana Green received this word for a client on October 13, 2014, and we learned more about the breakthrough gate:

The power of the Father is released to extract and separate the mixture and make room for Him, which will make room for prophetic existence. It is now being restored—authority over the dimensions, soaring, exploring, obtaining treasures, learning to war, authority for transformation. It feels like the gate is at the focal point of the length, width, height and depth. The focal point seems to be a black hole where one has been sucked into the evil places. I feel the Power of the Father to pull you out, a power greater than the speed of light. This is the gate that leads to the original design and the origin where everything was created good. This is a recalibration. Who can stand against this?

The Hebrew word *peres*[7] is packed with meaning. It is a military word that means destruction but can also mean increase, as in the increase of produce and progeny. The result of the breakthrough is therefore a destruction of what has come against one, which leads to increase.

In Micah 2:13, we are instructed that it is the King who leads one out through the breakthrough gate. The Hebrew word king is *melek*, which is the first letters in Melchizedek, Jesus Christ, our High Priest.

It was now time for me to speak. I shared these insights with the congregation, and then invited them to walk out of their imprisonment and through the breakthrough gate into new areas of freedom. The results were dramatic. Surges of power came upon many of the individuals, as they experienced the miraculous power of our Lord.

Job 36:16 beautifully pictures what the Lord was doing:

> *Then indeed, He enticed you from the mouth of distress, instead of it, a broad place with no constraint; and that which was set on your table was full of fatness.*[8]

CHAPTER TEN

The Golden Pipes

While on a trip to Kaneohe, HI in October 2014, two friends had come for ministry during the last few hours of a two-day fast. Almost halfway through the ministry session with the first person I (Paul) felt, unexpectedly, both a spiritual shift and a pronounced burning sensation manifesting on the back of my head. It was as if someone had laid two vertical, parallel, burning hot rods on the rear of my head. Something drastic had happened to me.

For years, as I would begin a ministry session and connect with the client, I could physically feel the flow of evil coming off of the person as we prayed. In the early years I would discern the evil being removed for almost seventy-two hours. Then a major shift began, first with the revelation of the spiritual rulers and then with the spiritual beings called stars, as both the physical discernment and the length of time decreased. Another major swing took place with the revelation of Melchizedek; but now, with the appearance of these rods, I realized that I could no longer feel the deliverance at all.

When the second person arrived for prayer I was in a quandary, wondering what was I supposed to do, because the Lord gave me a sense that I was just to sit and allow Him to release His power. I shared my observation with her and she was content to allow the Lord to do what He wanted, saying, "I'm seeing a sphere around you. It encircles above your head 'till just under your knees. I'm seeing yellow, like a light honey color. It's a liquid. Oil. Like oil. Fluid. Moving. Not touching you. I can feel it when I run my hand over the surface."

I wrote the following observations during the session, as a friend added insights:

> The power of the Father; released to extract and separate the mixture and make room for Him, which will make room for (client's name) for prophetic existence. It is now being restored. Authority over the dimensions is soaring, exploring, and obtaining treasures; learning to war; it's authority for transformation.

> I feel like a gate is at the focal point of the length, width, height and depth and seems to be a black hole where one has been sucked into the evil places, as Jana's word indicated, and I feel the Power of the Father to pull you out, a power greater than the speed of light.

> I feel the Father as Power. This is the first gate that leads to the original design and the origin where everything was created good, the ancient doors and gates of Psalm 24.

> I feel the two pillars, Jachin and Boaz,[1] meaning 'He shall establish' and 'in His youth is strength'. It feels like Palmoni and it is vibrating at 444 Hz. These two are holy ones who are part of the judicial heavenly government. His throne is established on justice and righteousness. Recalibration. Feels like the wrath of the Lamb. Who can stand against this?

The session was over and I was alone with Rob Gross and Larry and Jacqueline Pearson. We could all feel the rods on the back of our heads burning. I had contacted Jana Green and she immediately saw what looked like golden rods on the back of my head, mounted on what looked like a black fence-like structure, which I felt was some type of electrical insulation. Between the two rods she could see an electrical current arcing.

The next day the client contacted me and said that the chronic hip and knuckle pain she had suffered with had disappeared. I was stunned, because we had not even prayed about this pain. I also had a sobering feeling, a sense of awe, reverence, and fear of the Lord. What power this was! If I was aware of this power, was the enemy also aware of this new display of the presence of God? At some point I remember asking the Lord, "Is this Your Glory?" "Yes," He replied. "Is this your Love?" "Yes," again. What an insight! His Love is His Power! So I asked, "Was this a manifestation of your Power?" "Yes."

I could not help feeling that if this Power was displayed in the heavenly places, then the enemy must realize the significance of the Power, and the implications were clear. Nothing in the heavenly places or on earth could stand against this Power of God. Would this not cause panic in the camp of the enemy, and would this not result in demonic strategies to counter what God was doing?

The following day several of us gathered for prayer in the evening. Larry Pearson gave us new insight as the Lord spoke to him regarding His plan to bestow Power upon a new generation:

> We are being qualified to carry great Power. He's re-calibrating something in order to carry the Power. There's a conductor being put in us to carry Power.

> "You'll carry My greatness to the nations. The greatness of My Power will shift and bring great showers of blessing, glory and life. Where there is death, there shall be life. The rulers are here and they've drawn near to see

the emerging generation of Power. A Power generation will birth in the nation and the nations. Clarity will come with the spirit of understanding to build with Me. I'm establishing gates of Power in strategic places in this hour. They will be My outposts that will send forth the signals for the coming angelic army. There is coming a higher rank of spiritual beings to unlock mysteries, inventions, and creations of a different kind. The Angel of the Harvest is here. Everything is shifting. The platelets are shifting in the foundation of My temple. Time to get ready. Time to be steady with the things of My heart. I am releasing a wind that will set apart the mind of man from the things of My heart. The harvest is ready. It is time to see whom I have made ready to return to Me. Not with their garments, but with their heart. Behold, I come as Power. The wind of change is at hand. I desire to redeem the land and cover it with My hand for My moving will be grand. That which I have promised I will bring to flourishing. It is a generation of hope and a generation that will stand to proclaim that the land is the Lord's, and the fullness thereof. Supernatural rain will fall like torrents and heal, many to be prepared to call in the multitudes. It is time to take a step, and be bold and be strong, for the winds will not harm you but empower you to live from above and not from beneath. I am about to unsheathe My sword and take off the head of that which exalts itself. A new breed of leadership is being born."[2]

Jana Green, at home in California, continued to hear from the Lord:

I am experiencing very specific discernment. My fingers are going off again with that arch between the thumb and first finger. Paul and Larry are a generating connection of apostolic and prophetic power. The Eye of the Lord is intense. I feel this is connected to El Shaddai, the God who sees.

"Once again I have established a platform of justice, a place confirmed for judgment. It's not against what is creative, lovely or pure, but against the unbelief of My people and the injustices...Set your face as flint against the enemy of My elect. This reformation of change is assured from a heart of the original self; it will be true to endure. My hammer of justice will break the stronghold of indifference at the gate. For the lack of passion, true love has been denied. Delight in the Lord, then your desires of the heart will recreate and thrive. It's time for the resurrection from apathy to accrue. Their desires from the deep will be heard. Now Mercy and Truth stand at this gate to bring forth abundance in this place. The re-creative Power will reveal to align My people to be free from fear."

On Thursday, we began our weekend training, fully aware of the constant burning on the back of our heads. Revelation continued to unfold. We could now feel the rods extending way above our heads, and also down our backs and legs into the ground. At times we would feel what seemed to be electrical currents moving up and down the rods. Surges of Power would travel along the rods in such an overpowering way that we were overwhelmed by the Power.

As I have often said, revelation always comes in the context of other believers. As we shared what we were experiencing with the people in the seminar, a colonel in the US Army commented that the Lord had just told him that we were discerning transducers, explaining that a transducer changes one form of energy into another form. For example, a microphone is a transducer that changes sound energy into electrical energy. A transducer also measures the flow of energy. So what did this all mean?

During the entire time of this unfolding revelation there was an underlying drama taking place in Hawaii. Hurricane Anna was headed for the leeward side of the Islands and, instead of the hurricane weakening as usually happens, the storm was intensifying in strength. It was expected to hit Oahu on Saturday night and into Sunday. It appeared that a major catastrophe was about to take place, but as the storm slowly approached and intensified in strength, it also started drifting away from the islands. By Sunday morning, the storm was well over 160 miles off the leeward side, and only a gentle rain fell in Kaneohe as I preached. We were overcome by the prophetic nature of what was transpiring.

'Anna' means grace. Surely God's grace had been extended toward us. Pondering Jana's word and the revelation received, we recognized that the hurricane is a whirlwind that moves in a counter clockwise direction and brings destructive power, yet the effect of this hurricane on us was a wonderfully gentle rain. Although we were not in the eye of the storm, we were experiencing the calmness of the eye. As I preached that morning, I said, "Look outside. Notice how wonderful the rain is yet there is not even a leaf moving! There is no wind, yet this rain is from the hurricane."

Since Tuesday, when the rods on the back of my head appeared, they had burned so powerfully that I was often in pain. I noticed that the rods would burn more strongly at some times than others. One day Rob and another friend went with me to a Thai restaurant for lunch. As I walked in, I could feel the pipes rising in power and wondered what was going on now. We sat down and ordered. Then the Thai owner, who Rob had never met, came out from the back, fetched a chair and sat down at our table. She began to share with us all the pain her life. Though surprised, all of us at the table began ministering to her and praying for her. We had not initiated the conversation; she had. Was this a display of the Power of these rods?

I also noticed that we have entered into a new realm of protection. Since the discernment of these rods began, I am no longer aware of evil around me. If I get into a situation where evil is present, I feel the rods burning with surges of power. It is like there is now a force field of security around me.

After returning home, I continued to recognize that prayer ministry had changed. Pondering what all of this could mean, I kept asking the Lord if there was a biblical name for these rods and this power. The Lord did not disappoint, but nevertheless I was shocked when I realized that they were the golden pipes in Zechariah 4:11-12:

> *I answered and said to him, "What are these two olive trees—at the right of the lampstand and at its left?" And I further answered and said to him, "What are these two olive branches that drip into the receptacles of the two gold pipes from which the golden oil drains?"*

Reading the passage, I used discernment and could feel the two olive trees on either side of me, the bowl on top of my head, and the branches that drip the oil into the bowls. Zechariah 4 begins with a description of the two trees:

> *Now the angel who talked with me came back and wakened me, as a man who is wakened out of his sleep. And he said to me, "What do you see?" So I said, "I am looking, and there is a lampstand of solid gold with a bowl on top of it, and on the stand seven lamps with seven pipes to the seven lamps. Two olive trees are by it, one at the right of the bowl and the other at its left.*[3]

This is the imagery. There are two olive trees, and on each tree is a branch, which could most likely be translated as a spike—meaning the end of the branch. The oil goes from that spike to the bowl, from which there are seven spigots that fuel the seven lamps, which are the seven eyes of the Lord.

Drawing by Jana Green, *http://www.signsandwondersstudio.com*

As you read Zechariah 4 it is clear that Zechariah is being told something about Power. Perhaps this is the Power of the Spirit through the pipes.

> *So he answered and said to me: "This is the word of the Lord to Zerubbabel: 'Not by might nor by power, but by My Spirit,' Says the Lord of hosts."* [4]

The Hebrew word 'pipe' is *santerot*. In a *Journal of Hebrew Studies* article, Al Wolters explores the meaning of the word. He believes that the *santerot* are spiritual beings and that the correct translation of pipes should be 'pressers of gold.' He would translate Zechariah

4:12 as, "Who are these two spikes of the olive trees, which are in the hands of the two pressers of gold—the ones who express the gold from (the olives) on them."

Through discernment I can add that these two olive trees seem to be spiritual beings called powers.[5] The golden pipes also appear to be another pair of living beings called powers. During a coaching session, I experimented with a compass to see if the golden pipes were electromagnetic. I had a person hold the compass and I got down onto my knees and moved under the compass. Each time I did this the needle on the compass would move. Evidentially these pipes are magnetic.

Between the two olive trees there is the golden candlestick,[6] made up of seven lamps, which are the seven eyes of the Lord,[7] mistakenly called the seven chakra points by the New Age movement. The seven eyes of the Lord are tied to the Seven Spirits of God mentioned in Isaiah 11:2.

We have now reached a point where further revelation is needed. It seems that the power that is being released by the Lord through the two olive trees is used to fuel the seven eyes of the Lord. We need to understand more about these seven eyes.

The golden pipes continue to burn…

CHAPTER ELEVEN

Windows and Branches

In January 2015, I (Paul) woke up on my birthday and remembered a dream in which I was looking at an open window to my left, and wondering why it was open. Through the screen, I could see a tree branch rapidly growing and branching out. I looked outside to my right and saw another branch growing.

Less than a month later, I had another dream. Looking through two windows in a warehouse, I could see two cabins, and realized I had rented the cabin on the left. I went to the cabin and met a caretaker who said I was to check out at 6:00 AM. Realizing it was now 9:00 AM I thought, "What a stupid time to check out!" The caretaker said, "Since you are late you owe one thousand times for each minute you were late."

I was stunned. Even after all these years of generational prayer, evidentially I had not recognized something that was profoundly affecting me, to the extent that the enemy still had a right to exact a huge penalty against me.

The Lord has been showing us that there are not only gates and doors in the heavenly places, but also windows. A familiar passage in Malachi 3:10-11 teaches us about these windows:

> *Bring all the tithes into the storehouse,*
> *That there may be food in My house,*
> *And try Me now in this,"*
> *Says the LORD of hosts,*
> *"If I will not open for you the windows of heaven*
> *And pour out for you such blessing*
> *That there will not be room enough to receive it.*
> *"And I will rebuke the devourer for your sakes,*
> *So that he will not destroy the fruit of your ground,*
> *Nor shall the vine fail to bear fruit for you in the field,"*
> *Says the LORD of hosts.*

In my dream, I realized that the open windows should not have been open, and it seemed to be tied to my generational line. The mother's side seemed to be on the left, and the father's on the right. Isaiah 24:18 and Joel 2:9 speak of open windows that result in severe problems:

> *And it shall be*
> *That he who flees from the noise of the fear*
> *Shall fall into the pit,*
> *And he who comes up from the midst of the pit*
> *Shall be caught in the snare;*
> *For the windows from on high are open,*
> *And the foundations of the earth are shaken.*
>
> *They run to and fro in the city, they run on the wall; they climb into*
> *the houses, they enter at the windows like a thief.*

It seems we have often looked at Malachi 3:10-11 only in the context of tithing, but not in the larger context of the chapter, which lists many sins that can have generational impact.

In the first dream, I realized that ungodly windows were still open above me, not only because of my sin but also because of generational iniquity. The second dream indicated that the enemy, the caretaker, was exacting a severe financial penalty because of these open windows. I also realized that instead of renting that house, I should be the owner.

Other truths were to be discovered in the dream as well. What was the brilliant white branch that I saw growing so rapidly, and branching out? Although Joel 1:7 indicates a white branch that was stripped and made white, it seemed that the branch I saw was a righteous branch that was not correctly connected to me. Jesus said He is the vine and we are the branches, and in the Old Testament, Jesus is referred to as the Branch (Zechariah 4:8, Isaiah 11:1). It seems that because of generational and lifetime sin, we are not correctly connected as a branch to The Branch, Jesus. Instead, ungodly branches have been connected to us, which need to be destroyed so we can be rightly connected to Jesus, the True Branch. It appears that these branches connect us through the heavenly windows to the gates and the doors in the heavenly places.

On June 9, 2015, Chuck Pierce released this prophecy:

> As you are praising, arise out of the depth of your hearts. My windows are opening up even now in a greater way than you've ever experienced. So prepare your house for the multiplication of people, the multiplication of resources, the multiplication of success, the multiplication of My presence. For I have glorious benefits that you know not of. Prepare yourself for the glorious benefits that I will be sending your way!

> Port cities, prepare yourselves! For even now I will re-arrange the trade structures that are being brought in. I will re-arrange the way you are doing things, and I will bring some new ships in. There will be an uncovering of what is being brought into this nation. I am re-aligning

the trade routes. Watch the hurricanes this year as they form. For as the hurricanes are now beginning to form in Heaven during this 'whirlwind' year, you will now see the movement of these hurricanes come into earth by August. And you'll see a movement and new routes and alignments begin to form."

To review, in October 2014, we were in Kaneohe, Hawaii as Hurricane Anna moved toward Hawaii, and we were preparing for the landfall of the storm. During the week before the expected arrival of the storm, the Lord had revealed the golden pipes and the whirlwind through discernment (Zechariah 4). The following weekend Anna (grace) turned slightly away from the Islands, and Oahu was blessed with gentle rainfall but no hurricane-force winds. We learned a powerful lesson; when we are in His Eye and surrounded by the righteous whirlwind, we are protected by His grace. We also moved into a new understanding of His Power. Now it was July 2015, and I was stunned by Chuck Pierce's word because it was exactly nine months to the day that remnants of another hurricane brought historic rains to Southern California. Torrential rains fell in the High Desert where we live. What was conceived in Hawaii was birthed in Southern California. The desperately needed blessing of rain in drought-stricken Southern California had fallen! I believe this is an indication that revival has come to the Pacific Coast.

Those nine months indicate that when we understand the windows and branches, we are linked to His blessings, grace, and power in the fullness of His time. So, how do we move from where we have been to a new place of experiencing the power and the blessings of open heavenly windows?

My dream was a roadmap. I needed to pray and ask the Lord to reverse some issues in my generational line and me so that the righteous windows of heaven could be opened, and so that I could be correctly connected by the righteous branches to The Branch, Jesus, and to the heavenly places. As we discussed these concepts with many people, the Lord gave us a prayer. As you pray, it is my prayer that you will experience His Power and the blessings of heaven.

CHAPTER TWELVE

Prayer Renouncing Illegal Access of the Windows of Heaven

Lord, on behalf of my family line as well as myself, I submit this prayer. I lay claim to the heavenly world court case against the enemy that occurred on February 5, 2015 at Aslan's Place in Apple Valley, CA. I ask You to enforce the judgments made against the enemy on that day, and to close all windows that need to be closed and open all windows that need to be opened. Lord, remove any ungodly branches and totally graft me into You as a branch in Your vine. I declare that You are the true vine and I am a branch of You. Please remove all ungodly branches and burn them. I repent for establishing and nurturing these ungodly branches, and for not acknowledging you as My true vine and myself as a branch on Your vine.

Father, in the name of Jesus, I ask You to forgive us for illegally accessing the windows of heaven for the purpose of personal financial gain. I repent for and renounce opening any heavenly windows through occult practice, idolatry, divination, witchcraft, covenant breaking, ungodly trading, the exploitation of others and false religions. I also repent for closing windows that should not be closed. Please close every window, gate and door that we opened illegally, and open every window, gate and door that should not have been closed.

Lord, please take me back to the womb of the dawn[1] and recreate my DNA and RNA so that any influence of the fallen sons of God in my DNA and RNA is totally removed.

Lord, please remove all ungodly roots and branches.

Lord, I repent for not aligning to Your times and seasons to open and close windows. I repent for building my own times in reference to the windows. I repent for interrupting the flow of God's times. I repent for extending times when they should not be extended.

I repent for defiling and making the windows dirty. Father, please clean the windows in the generational line and cleanse me now by the blood of Your Son, setting me free from the consequences of opening heavenly windows by illegal means. Lord, You stated in John 14:6 that You are the way, the truth and the life and that no one can access the heavenly realms except through You. Please close every window, every door and every gate that was opened illegally, and restore us to Your plumb line. From this day forward, I will enter the windows of heaven only though You, as Your Spirit leads.

Lord, take the ax to the ungodly root in the ungodly womb of the dawn and destroy all ungodly roots and branches. Rightly connect me to Your roots, branches, and vine so that I can function as a godly branch in the order of Melchizedek. Please give me a new heart.

I repent for any ungodly way in which we accessed windows. Please apply the scarlet thread, the hyssop, and the cedar[2] to all ungodly covenants that opened windows that should not be open, and remove all access that ungodly stars gained because of those ungodly covenants in my family line. I repent for all ungodly covenants that affected any land area. Please disconnect us from those land areas.

Please break all ungodly ties to time, and to the windows of time and times. I repent for ungodly access to time, times and half of time, and ask You to apply Your blood to all markers in time. Please restore godly boundaries between space and time, and close all ungodly windows and doors between time and space. I repent for any way that we accessed time through space, or space through time.

Please break off ungodly connections between stars and time. I repent for making all ungodly calendars based on the cycles of time and for changing times and seasons, and declare that all my days are written in Your book.

Please remove the abomination of desolation off of my family line, and remove all generational pages of the enemy that have been inserted into my book.

I repent for those who did not understand that the tithe was to go to Melchizedek, to Jesus, our High Priest. I repent for giving according to my own desires or due to the pressure of others, rather than asking Melchizedek, Jesus, our High Priest where I am to give my tithe.

As I am conceived in the womb of the dawn, do not allow any parts of me to be influenced by the fallen sons of God, or stars, or any other fallen spiritual beings. Please do not allow any animal, plant, fish, or spiritual DNA and RNA to be weaved into my DNA and RNA. Please remove any unholy sequencing in my DNA and RNA placed there by the fallen sons of God. In the womb of the dawn, please correctly sequence the ACGT coding of my original design in the conception replication of all my DNA and RNA.

At my birth from the womb of the dawn, do not allow me to be scattered, but establish the righteous pillars of wisdom. Melchizedek, the true Lord Jesus, do not allow me to be scattered in the stars and in other time periods. I do not agree with that. Please do not allow any parts of me to be scattered in the unholy height, depth, length and width, or in all unholy dimensions and kingdoms.

I repent for those in my family and tribe who, by majority, made agreements with the enemy that ended up entrapping me even though it was not my desire.

At conception, please establish the correct lightning strikes to fuse my spirit to my soul and body. Please breathe into me so I am a living soul according to Your original desire and not according to the plans of the enemy.

Lord, as my spirit is moving from Your throne, please guide me so that I go to the holy height, depth, length and width; and prohibit any effort of the enemy to capture me and place me or any parts of me in the unholy depth, length, width, and height. I lay claim to all repentance and renunciations that I have prayed, that the enemy may not be allowed to capture me.

Lord, please remove all unholy subscripts from my generational line that allowed unholy authorities to carry curses down my generational line. Please disconnect me from the ungodly library, ungodly scrolls, the ungodly librarian, and all ungodly knowledge.

In the name of Jesus Christ, I repent for nurturing humanistic mindsets. I repent for placing the standards of man at a higher priority than Your truth.

I repent for times I allowed personal decisions to override Your leadership and truth. Lord, I ask that You now disassemble and clean off all false and ungodly branches.

Please clean all Godly branches, close all windows that should be closed, and do the same for all gates and doors.

Please remove all influence from Chronos time, and bring me into Your full Kairos time.

Please burn and destroy all that You are cleaning off.

Lord, I ask You now to release Your Power.

CHAPTER THIRTEEN
The Greatest Power

If you are reading this my wife, Donna, has agreed to the use of this chapter to finalize our book about the Power of God on earth as it is in heaven. This is easily the most difficult chapter I have ever written. Yes, I used the word 'easily' and 'difficult' in the same sentence.

I was so frustrated! Doing all I knew to do, and agreeing to all I thought I could agree to, I felt as if I could do no more but from my perspective it was not enough. What more could I do? My only solution was to take my nightly dip in our Jacuzzi and go to bed. I eased into the hot water and issued my complaint, "Lord, I understand Donna is in a lot of pain and she is relating to me through the lens of pain medication, but I do not know what to do. Everything I do or say seems to be wrong; I am having difficulty communicating with Donna; I say something and it seems to be misinterpreted; there seems to be no solution..." I was numb, convinced that there was no answer, convinced that nothing would ever change, but I was not prepared for how the Lord would respond.

In my despair, I heard Him clearly ask, "Do you understand how much Donna has suffered because of what you do?" I was immediately taken back by the Lord's words, and our lives together as a married couple of forty-plus years raced through my memory. I finally understood.

Donna and I were married at the First Baptist Church of Downey, California in 1968, where after returning from our honeymoon we began serving as Junior High sponsors. At the same time, I was teaching eighth grade at Baldwin Park Unified School District in Southern California. In 1971, I resigned from the teaching position and began working full time at the church. For almost 7 years we enjoyed a wonderful time of ministry with the youth during what later was to be called the Jesus Movement. Our pastor, Harold Adams, protected the staff of this 2,000-member church from the political drama of church life. We literally were unaware of the tensions that often accompany the organizational life of a large church. These years were filled with joy as our children were born, and we experienced the satisfying delight of church life with many friends. We also enjoyed many wonderful holidays with our parents, who not only were also members of our church, but who had also become friends. Looking back, we now realize it was idyllic life that we enjoyed.

The pull to become a senior pastor became stronger and stronger, until finally Donna and I agreed that this was where the Lord was leading. Though I can honestly say I did not want to leave Downey First Baptist, we accepted the call to pastor a Baptist church in Idaho in 1977. The heartaches began.

Moving far away from family and friends, we were still excited to begin pastoring the church. Before long, Donna received an invitation from a woman in the church to come to her house. I was so excited, but my elation was very short lived when she came home almost destroyed. The visit turned out to be a time for complaints and of criticisms against the new pastor's wife, who was informed that her clothes were not appropriate, and that she should stand at the back door with me after the morning worship service to shake hands with the parishioners. Her loneliness and isolation became intense. We loved the people of the church and they loved us, but the realities of pastoring and the unreasonable expectations of church members toward Donna were real and unfair. It was in Idaho that she began having physical issues tied to the stress of being a pastor's wife.

In 1980, we moved to Montclair, CA and accepted the position of senior pastor of a 450-member church. Because our salary was not sufficient, Donna found it necessary to work outside the home. We had wonderful years of ministry there, experiencing the normality of life, raising three children, and serving the church in cooperation with the larger American Baptist family. This all changed in 1989, after our first prayer session for deliverance. The church divided into two camps, those excited about what the Lord was doing and those who resisted the demonstration of the Power of God. It was much easier for me than Donna, because as the tension increased, it was difficult for her to hear the words that were spoken against me. Finally in 1991, the church had a series of meetings where accusations were brought, and after one meeting Donna was in so much agony that she refused to get in the car and insisted on walking home. She could not be consoled. A week later, after another difficult meeting, I made the decision to resign. Donna's grief could not be measured.

The leadership of the American Baptist Churches of the Pacific Southwest was very kind to us, and a position as an interim pastor was offered. As I traveled to San Diego on Sunday mornings and returned Wednesday night, we also began a church in Chino, California. A man who had been in junior high during our time at Downey First Baptist became excited about what the Lord was doing and decided to join us in the new church plant. He, his wife, and two children moved in with us. It would be impossible to describe how dreadful the time was for Donna. With me gone from Sunday through Wednesday, she was left to manage the house, this family, and her mother who was suffering with renal failure. The family seemed delighted to have someone to take care of them, and it was a constant struggle to get them to help around the house.

In 1992, we met another pastor and eventually we were invited to join his church where I became his co-pastor. For two years we enjoyed wonderful ministry again, but that would all change in 1994. Sin issues were exposed in my co-pastor's life, and the elders and I were confronted the difficult decision to remove him from his position. The church went into turmoil, and Donna again suffered as she endured allegations coming against me. After all was said and done, the church voted not to retain me as pastor, but failed to remove my designation as co-pastor, so I felt released to resign, and we were again unemployed. Donna had lost another church family and many friends.

After pursuing the Lord's direction, we became convinced we were to move to the high desert of Southern California to pastor a church in Apple Valley. Because the church could not fully support us, I returned to teaching as a substitute, and Donna began working again. The church eventually was able to pay me a fulltime salary, but that was short lived. Understanding that I needed to find another job and realizing I could not pastor and work at the same time, I resigned from the church.

Throughout these years, the Lord continued to train me in deliverance and discernment, but now we wondered if my ministry would continue. Both Donna and I became depressed, thinking that, perhaps, ministry was over for us. Finances were tight, we were unable to fulfill the lease option on our home in Apple Valley, and we also found it necessary to do a short sale on our house in Montclair. Unable to find a place to rent, we moved in with a college student who had a large house. Donna, who had raised our kids in our own home, now found herself without a place of her own. More pain.

After a short time we moved into a rental, and the Lord opened the door to join a ministry in Idyllwild, California. Because of the small living space we sold or gave away almost everything we had collected during our lifetime of raising our children—more loss for Donna.

We had only been in Idyllwild a few months when Donna told me, "This is not going to work here." I could not believe her! We had just moved, but she was right, and before one year was finished the Lord opened another door. In 1999, we moved to Hesperia, CA and Aslan's Place began. Although we had moved into another new and great adventure, Donna again experienced the loss of more relationships.

Ministry exploded and we traveled extensively. Then in 2001, everything changed again. During a ministry trip to Minneapolis, Donna was suddenly overcome with pain in her side, which increased during the following years until she required massive doses of pain medication. Our HMO refused to act swiftly to determine the source of the pain, and it was a very long time before it was diagnosed as sludge in the biliary duct. She was healed for a while but then the pain soon returned. Constant trips to the doctor became the norm for years, and several procedures were performed to relieve her pain. In one attack alone, she had seven ERCP's.[1]

During these difficult years, several different manipulative women came in our lives, becoming very close to Donna. Seeming to be friends, they pulled on her and her gift of mercy, attempting to gain attention for themselves. One of our true friends saw that these women were carving pieces out of Donna for their own benefit, using the phrase 'melon balling' to describe her insight.

Ministry constantly increased during the years of Donna's pain. I remember once I complained to the Lord that I could not take care of my wife and still minister, but the Lord clearly spoke to me, "You are not to say that again!" I understood, and realized that I could love my wife, take care of her, and still minister by making some changes and ministering from home via Skype and the phone.

Three times after moving to the high desert, Donna developed chest pain in the area of her heart. We would call 911, and ambulances would come and take her to the hospital for treatment and testing, but no heart issues could be found. In retrospect, we have realized that Donna was reacting physically to spiritual advancements that were taking place in the ministry.

Then the worse crisis in my life with Donna happened. Hospitalized once again for constant pain and a supposed heart condition, she had received massive doses of medication and had become delusional. In her confusion, she was convinced I had put her in a psychiatric ward. She insisted that she no longer wanted me as her pastor, and I was fired. I was stunned! I remember going home, totally disheartened. I had loved Donna with all my heart. Many times in the midst of her suffering I had told her I would give up ministry and find a regular job, and I meant it. I would prefer her over ministry. I would love her unconditionally. Now, despite my deep love of her and my loving actions toward her, I found myself realizing that this kind of love was not enough. I prayed quietly, "Lord, if this love is not enough, then who can truly love? Is it at all possible?" That night, during troubled sleep, I wondered what would happen to our lives. Fortunately, Donna called the first thing in the morning to apologize. It really was the fog of medication, but it been a night of soul-searching agony for me as I questioned the Lord about the issue of love, as the memories cascaded through my mind that night in the Jacuzzi. Donna had suffered tremendously because of the call on my life, and it wasn't over.

There were still more years of side pain ahead, but we finally reached a point when it seemed to have been healed. Feeling good, Donna attended a conference we were conducting, where she fell, shattering her shoulder and resulting in more years of pain before a shoulder replacement finally resolved the issue.

Much to our dismay, once the shoulder was healed, the side pain returned again. In April 2014, the doctor told Donna he would not be able to increase the pain medication so this is what life would look like now—constant pain. All I could do was declare in faith, "God was good and His love endures forever." I would need to adjust my life again so I could take care of Donna, but then God intervened.

While at Aslan's Place on May 10, 2014, the Lord revealed a trinity of evil over the high desert. At His direction, we prayed and discerned a huge deliverance coming off of the land. I went home to find that Donna was pain free. The Lord had healed her too! Some months later, the pain returned briefly, but again the Lord revealed some territorial issues and when He freed that land, the pain in Donna's side gradually disappeared.

What have I learned though all of this? There is one command that the Lord gives to husbands. We are called to love our wives as Christ loves the church. No, not just called; we are commanded to love our wives. Look at Ephesians 5:25:

> *Husbands, love your wives, just as Christ loved the church and gave Himself for her…*

The word 'love' is in the imperative. It is a command. Notice we are not commanded to minister, but loving your wife is a command. I learned that Donna is to be first after my love of the Lord. Ministry is secondary to the unconditional love I am to have for my wife.

Since 1989, I have experienced the wonder of the Power of God. I have often found myself glued to the floor by His Power. I have felt His Power on my body, but all this demonstration of His Power is not His greatest Power. His greatest Power is His love for us, and the greatest power we can demonstrate is our love for one another.

> *In this the love of God was manifested toward us, that God has sent His only begotten Son into the world, that we might live through Him. In this is love, not that we loved God, but that He loved us*

and sent His Son to be the propitiation for our sins. Beloved, if God so loved us, we also ought to love one another.[2]

The reality is that we cannot love like this. It is Christ in us, His powerful love coming through us to others. He is the Greatest Power of Love.

For this reason I bow my knees to the Father of our Lord Jesus Christ, from whom the whole family in heaven and earth is named, that He would grant you, according to the riches of His glory, to be strengthened with might through His Spirit in the inner man, that Christ may dwell in your hearts through faith; that you, being rooted and grounded in love, may be able to comprehend with all the saints what is the width and length and depth and height—to know the love of Christ which passes knowledge; that you may be filled with all the fullness of God.[3]

ENDNOTES

INTRODUCTION

[1] Throughout this book 'Power' is capitalized when in reference to God's Power to reinforce the fact that this is God's Power alone, except as quoted directly from scripture.

[2] John 21:25

[3] Ephesians 1:17-21

CHAPTER 1: *Pondering The Power Of God*

[1] 1 Samuel 5

[2] 1 Samuel 6:8-9

[3] 1 Samuel 6:19-20

[4] 2 Samuel 6

[5] Luke 17:20-21

[6] Matthew 12:28

[7] John 5: 19

[8] John 12: 49

[9] Luke 4:14

[10] Luke 4:36

[11] Luke 5:17

[12] John 14:12

[13] Acts 1:8

[14] Ephesians 3:7

[15] Ephesians 3:20-21

CHAPTER 2: *Power, On Earth As It Is In Heaven*

[1] 1 Corinthians 6:19

[2] Matthew 13:44

[3] Luke 17:20-22

[4] Matthew 6:9-13

[5] Matthew 3: 1-3

[6] Mark 9:1

[7] Mark 6:4

[8] Romans 1:16

[9] Matthew 10:1

[10] Mark 3:14-15

[11] Romans 14:17

[12] Romans 15:13

[13] Acts 17:24,26-28

[14] John 14:16-21

CHAPTER 3: *The Gift Of Tongues*

[1] Acts 2:4

[2] 1 Corinthians 14:21-22

[3] I am not sure if the same spiritual being brings the tongue and interpretation or if there are two different spiritual beings

[4] 1 Chronicles 16:23

[5] 1 Corinthians 14:6-18

[6] Episode 17 can be viewed at http://aslansplace.com/ehp-season1/

[7] Brian Cox, Paul's son, is a prayer minister and an administrator at Aslan's Place. In addition to many other tasks he manages the website and produces the webinars.

[8] Jana Green is an artist, a prayer minister, and a prophetic intercessor. Her website is http://www.signsandwondersstudio.com

[9] Tobias Renken is a long-time friend and prophetic intercessor for Aslan's Place. He lives in Germany.

[10] Paul discerns gifts as a flow coming off a person's body at different levels that correlate with the seven eyes of the Lord: forehead/teaching, eyes/prophetic, mouth/exhortation, shoulders/administration, heart/mercy, elbows/giving, hands/serving

[11] Isaiah 26:12

[12] Malachi 3:16

[13] 1 Corinthians 14:18-19

CHAPTER 4: *Tongues Of Men And Angels*

[1] Isaiah 28:14-18

[2] 1 Corinthians 13:1

[3] Acts 2:3

[4] Genesis 11:4

[5] https://en.wikipedia.org/wiki/Tower_of_Babel

[6] *Exploring Heavenly Places, Volume 3* discusses gates, doors and the grid

[7] 1 Corinthians 14:2

[8] 1 Corinthians 14:26

CHAPTER 5: *Power For Living, Power For Dying*

[1] John 15:33

[2] Ephesians 6

[3] *The Holy Bible, English Standard Version.* (2001). (Romans 8:38-39). Wheaton, IL: Crossway.

[4] Ephesians 6:10-13

[5] Psalm 107:14, 29-30

[6] Luke 15:7, 10

[7] Philippians 4:6-7

[8] Psalm 116:15

[9] 1 Corinthians 15:54

CHAPTER 6: *Unfolding Revelation Of God's Power*

[1] http://www.shemitah-blood-moons.net

[2] http://www.timeanddate.com/eclipse/blood-moon.html

[3] http://www.lindseywilliams.net/lindsey-williams-september-

2015-dates-of-significance/

[4] Matthew 11:28-30

[5] See *Exploring Heavenly Places, Volume 4* for an in-depth discussion of rainbows and an introduction to rainbow angels.

[6] Anthony Huselbus is a longtime friend of Aslan's Place, and a prophetic intercessor.

[7] Isaiah 28:14-17

[8] Isaiah 54:10, 17b

CHAPTER 7: *Puzzling Pieces*

[1] Mimi Lowe is a prayer minister, an author, and a board member of Joel's Well Ministries. Her website is http://www.mimilowe.com

[2] Dale Shannon is a professional life coach, college professor and prayer minister. Her website is http://www.fulfillyourdream.org

[3] Vector = Position, Direction, Speed, Coordinate. In vector calculus, a vector field is an assignment of a vector to each point in a subset of space. A vector field in the plane, for instance, can be visualized as a collection of arrows with a given magnitude and direction each attached to a point in the plane. Vector fields are often used to model, for example, the speed and direction of a moving fluid throughout space, or the strength and direction of some force, such as the magnetic or gravitational force, as it changes from point to point. In aviation a vector is the measure of the distance, direction (usually in degrees), the rate of flying and the point of origin in degrees… rate if flying… point of origin. http://en.wikipedia.org/wiki/Vector_field

CHAPTER 8: *The Missing Piece*

[1] Persis Tiner is a prayer minister, prophetic intercessor, and board member of Joel's Well Ministries

[2] Delta is change, and is also an electrical term for a three phase electrical system. http://en.wikipedia.org/wiki/Delta-v_%28physics%29

[3] I am not a math person, but for those who are, the following reference from http://www-math.mit.edu/~djk/calculus_beginners/chapter01/section02.html and might be helpful to explain the complexities of my dream. "Calculus is

the study of how things change. It provides a framework for modeling systems in which there is change, and a way to deduce the predictions of such models." (. Also, the relationship between the XYZ axis and vector force fields is analyzed at https://www.whitman.edu/mathematics/multivariable/multivariable_16_Vector_Calculus.pdf

[4] See *Exploring Heavenly Places, Volume 3* by Paul Cox and Barbara Parker for a discussion of gates, doors and the grid.

[5] In *Come Up Higher*, I wrote about the chessboard, which is made up of eight rows of eight, which totals 64 squares.

[6] See *Come Up Higher* by Paul L. Cox for a discussion about the *stoicheia*.

[7] It is interesting that a vector can also be used to describe a means for transporting a virus. Means of transport is vector.

[8] Even as this volume is being written, new revelation regarding the DNA and the elements of the periodic table is exploding and evidences of physical healing is being documents. Such late-breaking happenings are explored in the Exploring Heavenly Places webinars, and will be eventually find their way into this series. You can participate in the webinars live, or view them later. For more information, see http://aslansplace.com/webcast/

[9] See *Exploring Heavenly Places, Volume 2* by Paul Cox and Rob Gross for a discussion of the sons of God.

[10] Daniel 7:10

[11] Psalm 18:14

[12] Philippians 3:10

CHAPTER 9: *Breakthrough*

[1] Wilson, M. R. (1999). 1355 קָעַן. R. L. Harris, G. L. Archer Jr., & B. K. Waltke (Eds.), *Theological Wordbook of the Old Testament* (electronic ed.). Chicago: Moody Press.

[2] See *Exploring Heavenly Places, Volume 4: Power in the Heavenly Places*

[3] This would also include words spoken against oneself.

[4] Larry Pearson is co-founder of Lion Sword Communications. He is a co-founder and board member of Joel's Well Ministries. His website

is http://lionsword.ca

[5] Crystal Kain Ross is Barbara Parker's cousin and is a prophetic intercessor.

[6] Jude 12

[7] Hamilton, V. P. (1999). 1826 יָרַף. R. L. Harris, G. L. Archer Jr., & B. K. Waltke (Eds.), *Theological Wordbook of the Old Testament* (electronic ed.). Chicago: Moody Press.

[8] *New American Standard Bible*: 1995 update. (1995). (Job 36:16). LaHabra, CA: The Lockman Foundation.

CHAPTER 10: *The Golden Pipes*

[1] 1 Kings 7:21

[2] At this point, we knew Hurricane Anna was heading towards the Hawaiian Island and did not know that there would be only rain and no wind.

[3] Zechariah 4:1–3

[4] Zechariah 4:6

[5] See more about powers in *Heaven Trek* and *Come Up Higher*. Paul previously thought these two olive trees to be the Trees of Life (there is no indication that there was only one Tree of Life) but no longer believe this. It is possible the two trees are male and female, and that they are part of the trees of healing on either side of the River of God mentioned in Revelation?

[6] Paul also discerns the golden candlestick as a spiritual being called a power, from 'dunamis' in Greek

[7] Zechariah 4:10, Revelation 5:6

CHAPTER 11: *Prayer Renouncing Illegal Access Of The Windows Of Heaven*

[1] Psalm 110:3

[2] Multiple references in Leviticus 14

CHAPTER 12: *Love, The Ultimate Power*

[1] Endoscopic Retrograde Cholangiopancreatography
[2] 1 John 4:9-11
[3] Ephesians 3:14-19